James L. Shively
May 1992

SALMON FLIES

Salmon Flies

THEIR CHARACTER, STYLE, AND DRESSING

By Poul Jorgensen

Photographs by the Author

STACKPOLE BOOKS

SALMON FLIES

Copyright © 1978 by
Poul Jorgensen

Published by
STACKPOLE BOOKS
Cameron and Kelker Streets
P.O. Box 1831
Harrisburg, Pa. 17105

Published simultaneously in Don Mills, Ontario, Canada
by Thomas Nelson & Sons, Ltd.

Photo Credits: Photo of the author by Lefty Kreh. Photo on page 254 by Kris Lee.
Drawings by Bill Elliot.

Printed in the U.S.A.

Library of Congress Cataloging in Publication Data

Jorgensen, Poul.
  Salmon flies.

  Includes index.
  1. Fly tying. 2. Flies, Artificial.
3. Atlantic salmon fishing. I. Title.
SH451.J65 1978   688.7'9   78-17941
ISBN 0-8117-1426-8

To my children
Poul-Erik, Karen, and Peter

Contents

Foreword

Atlantic salmon flies and fishing combine to reach the zenith of the angling arts: the joining of delicate tackle with challenging techniques in casting the world's most beautiful flies in sturdy currents for the acknowledged king of fishes.

The beginning of fly fishing for salmon may have been in 1496, when Dame Juliana Berners' *Treatise Of Fishing With An Angle* was published. In it she mentioned salmon as well as trout, and she described a fly reminiscent of our popular March Brown. In those days, and for more than a hundred years hence, fly tackle was very crude, usually consisting of "poles," sixteen feet long or more, to which were attached plaited horsehair lines (without reels) and flies fashioned on reforged bent and barbed needles whipped onto the line.

By 1725 flies were made with eyes of twisted silkworm gut and, about then, various named patterns became popular due to books on angling written by ancient authors such as Walton, Chetham, and Bowlker. The first book showing salmon flies in color was by George Bainbridge in 1816. It contained a hand-colored engraving of five salmon flies, somber ones with dyed wool bodies and wings of turkey obtained mostly from birds raised for the purpose.

Then in 1845, the lid blew off!

A gillie named Jock dressed the fanciest fly ever seen for an angler named Scott while on the way by boat to a salmon river in Scandinavia. This gaudy confection of silks, feathers, and tinsel boasted herl butts veiled with toucan, a complicated mixed wing of colorful married strands of swan, and wing sections of several other birds, plus sides and cheeks of jungle cock and blue chatterer and horns of macaw—more than two dozen ingredients in all!

During the same year the invention of machinery afforded the quantity production of hooks with turned metal eyes instead of wrapped-on gut. It took more than fifty years for metal-eyed hooks to become widely accepted, and about fifty more for the old gut-eyed classics to be regarded as the rare collectors' items they now are.

Jock's famous fly, aptly named the Jock Scott, started a rivalry to see who could dress the gaudiest and most complicated patterns. They blossomed into thousands, of which a few still are popular, including such classics as the Green Highlander, Thunder and Lightning, Black Dose, and the four Doctors: Blue, Silver, Black, and Red. No conceivable combination of colors was left undone. Salmon struck them all, at least at one time or another, probably more because of form and presentation than because of beauty and complexity.

This era of the gaudy fly was Elizabethan, when British regiments and warships roamed the world. Nostalgic officers sent home rare plumages and were rewarded with gorgeously complicated salmon flies for use when they returned on leave. All this was aided and abetted by an angler-author named George Kelson, who in 1895 wrote a book called *The Salmon Fly* containing instructions for dressing about three hundred patterns, of which many were shown in color. Kelson had the unique impression that Atlantic salmon struck at butterflies, which may help to explain some of this. Regardless of how popular these gaudy flies were with the fish, they certainly pleased the fishermen, and they still are used to a minor extent.

After all these exquisite creations it was natural for more sensible authors to guide fly selection back into the range of common sense. This was done at the turn of the century principally by Ernest Crossfield, a great fly dresser who favored intentional translucence and no ornamentation without fishing value. The fancy flies didn't die all that quickly, but more and more anglers favored simpler ones such as the Blue Charm, Silver Blue, and Logie. All these flies, fancy as well as simple, were made with wings of feathers.

Now we jump to North America, where something else was going on. Here, anglers in general couldn't afford Kelson's classics or lacked the ability to dress them, regardless of ingredients available. They had to use whatever they had, which often was wool from an old sweater and the hair of animals such as cows, dogs, squirrels, or bear. They quickly found out that these crude hair wings outfished the fancy feathered ones, and the shift to hair wings began. Hair outfished feathers because it was more translucent. It breathed and pulsated in the water. When Sandy MacDonald in Nova Scotia, for example, came home with a salmon or two and was asked what he used to catch the fish, his answer might have been "with the Red Cow Fly"—or the Brown Dog, or Black Bear—everyone knew what he was talking about!

The classics weren't forgotten, however, but those that were used usually were simplified and made with wings of hair. Americans developed their own patterns, such as the Cosseboom, Red Abbey, and the famous Rat series. We still very successfully fish the Black Bear, for example, perhaps adding a butt of fluorescent green silk to the black-tinseled body and calling it the Green Butt.

Few fly dressers today are competent to dress the old classics because, given the ability, it takes years of practice to reach anything near perfection. As a collector of the ancient classics and their modern counterparts, and as a writer about them, I know of fewer than a dozen people in the world who could be said to have nearly or actually reached perfection. The work of these artists makes their reproductions of the classic patterns as collectible (and approximately as valuable) as the ancient gut-eyed gems of the Kelson era.

One of the few great artists is Poul Jorgensen, who offers you this book. I won't be so tactless as to say that Poul is the greatest, but I can say that he is the most versatile. He dresses salmon flies to near perfection, be they the complicated classics we treasure for show, or the simple hair wings we favor for fishing. He does just as well with his lifelike streamers, his delicate dry flies, and his nymphs that can all but crawl. I know other great specialists who excel in one way or another, but I know of no other who excels in so many of them.

Thus, this book was written by one of the world's greatest masters of the art of fly dressing. I hope it will challenge many of its readers to follow its author on the road toward perfection.

JOSEPH D. BATES, Jr.

Preface

Fly fishing for salmon is a tricky business. Success or failure is almost entirely dependent upon the performance of the fly, the angler's skill in presenting it to the fish, and, of course, the mood of the salmon. Unlike trout flies, which in most cases are dressed to imitate the many insects and larvae found on the stream, the salmon fly, with a few exceptions, does not represent anything in particular other than something the salmon will strike when the time and the river is "right."

Therefore, there are some things about salmon flies that are hard to explain. Perhaps it is the uniqueness of their character and style that makes them so easily recognizable among other flies, like rare stamps. Or perhaps it is their tradition and challenging complexity in dressing that fascinates us.

Not long ago when fishing for salmon on the Matapedia River in Quebec, Canada, my gillie, Henry Lyons, kept admiring the fully dressed flies I had brought with me for the occasion. "What a lovely fly," he said after I had tossed him a double-hook Dusty Miller for our next drop. "You know Poul, it's a shame that we don't see very many of those on the river any more." He continued to talk while tying the fly to the leader and dropping it over the side of the canoe to test its ability to swim the way he wanted it to.

He mumbled about forty-pound salmon, Green Highlanders, Jock Scotts, Black Doses, and Silver Greys. Finally he turned to me and said, "But I guess there are not very many left who can dress those anymore."

Henry was just as right about the current status of fly tying for salmon as he was when he explained that the lead fish had probably not yet reached the pool we were fishing, but that tomorrow, when rotation put us on Upper MacNeil, we would surely score. We did—twice, on the Dusty Miller.

It had been an encouraging week of salmon fishing. My conversations with Henry and other gillies and anglers were carried from the river to the evening warmth of the cabin where flies were being dressed for the following day. I am now more than ever convinced that individuals who suggest that feather-winged salmon flies are no longer needed or appreciated are in reality simply covering up their own inability to dress them.

I am also convinced, now more than ever, that a complete book on salmon fly dressing is needed so that the flies do not vanish completely. While it is true that there have been more books written on the subject of fly fishing and fly tying during the last ten years than in any other period in the history of the sport, we must admit that most of them were written for the trout fishermen, and justifiably so. A few of those books touch lightly on salmon flies, but none in any depth, and quite frankly, none of them brought the tyer to the point that after studying them one could say, "Now I can dress a salmon fly that incorporates all the fine traditions and specifications."

This book, however, is different. It is the first work in over sixty years that has been written exclusively about salmon flies and the contemporary methods of dressing both the old classics and the effective new patterns, such as the popular hair wings.

I hope this book will encourage the many fine fly tying instructors around the world who work with youngsters to teach them not only to dress the hair wings, but also the fine art of dressing the feather-wing salmon flies. In this way, the flies will not vanish, but live on for generations to enjoy. It is fitting that they be preserved in this way.

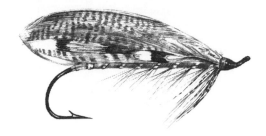

Acknowledgments

From the very moment an author draws the first outline for a book on any subject, up to the day of publication, he has used all the skill and knowledge at his disposal to cover his subject from one end of the spectrum to the other, and often relied on assistance from others. A book *is* hard work.

Since acknowledgments are usually the last pages to be written, this is the moment when I as author extend my gratitude to all the anglers and fly dressers too numerous to mention, who in one way or another gave me inspiration, taught me their tricks, and encouraged me to share with others. A very special thanks to my friend, the late William F. Blades, the fly-tier's fly-tier to whom I dedicated my first book, *Dressing Flies for Fresh and Salt Water,* and who is with me at the vise always — in spirit. I also wish to thank Jerry Hoffnagle and Neil McAleer of Stackpole Books and Eric Leiser of the Rivergate for their encouragement. Without them this book would not be before you. I am also very grateful to Bill Elliott, the noted wildlife artist, for the fine drawing of the salmon fly anatomy, and to my good friend and fishing companion Art Lee, a brilliant writer and salmon angler, for bringing me samples of flies from around the world. And to Joseph D. Bates, Jr., author of numerous books including the classic *Atlantic Salmon Flies and Fishing,* I express my sincere gratitude for writing the inspiring introduction.

And last, but certainly not least, a most heartfelt thanks to my good friend and companion Lefty Kreh, who is not only the world's foremost all-around fly angler, but also a magician in his darkroom, where the photos for this book were printed.

POUL JORGENSEN

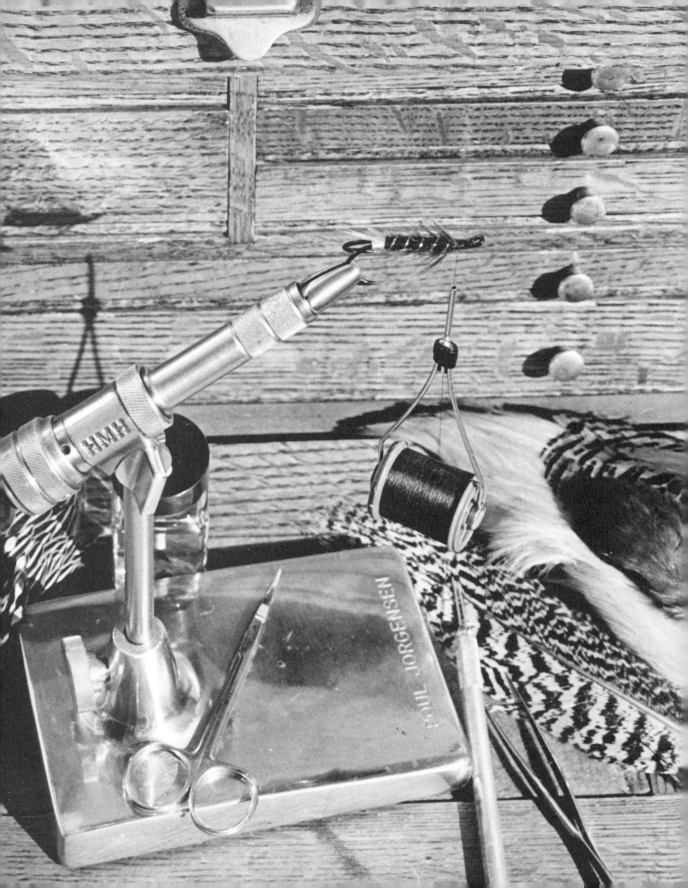

Tools, Hooks, and Materials

TOOLS

I have more than once remembered my good friend and tutor, the late Bill Blades, as he tried to describe the frustrating moments in the beginning of his fly tying days. "I tried to tie flies without a vise," he said, "but you know, it's a waste of time." Naturally, when something is considered a waste of time by the master himself, it must be tried. I soon discovered that it can be done as tiers of centuries ago had proven, but I could do it only on large hooks with satisfactory results. Therefore, I again use a vise, and I no longer tie salmon flies on gut-eyed hooks except, perhaps on rare occasions, for framing and display. However, I have always been an advocate of using as few tools as possible, and instead, I teach my fingers to do the job. The following tools are the *only* ones needed to tie good salmon flies; the rest is achieved by practice.

THE VISE

The vise is the most important tool in contemporary fly tying, and I highly recommend that you get the best your pocketbook will allow.

I have used Thompson's Model A vise for over twenty years and still have the first one I bought. It has a convenient lever action and adjustable jaws that make it easy to change from one hook size to another, even as large as a 3/0 salmon hook. It's available with a table clamp so that it can be adjusted up and

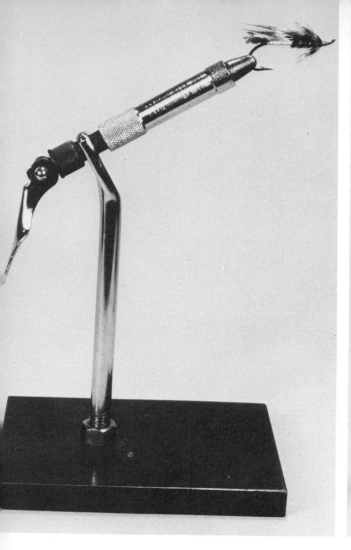

Thompson A vise with a metal base plate

The HMH vise on solid brass stand

down for a comfortable height, or mounted on a convenient base plate so that it can be used anywhere without having to rely on an edge for the clamp. But best of all, the head can be made to turn! This is particularly important when dressing salmon flies. With just a quarter turn the fly can be laid on the side without removing it, so that the left (far) side feathers can be positioned correctly before they are fastened on the shank (see photographs). The Thompson vise is still available from all better supply houses.

The HMH vise is undoubtedly the finest vise ever designed, a true Stradivarius for the discriminating fly dresser. It has a lever-operated mechanism to

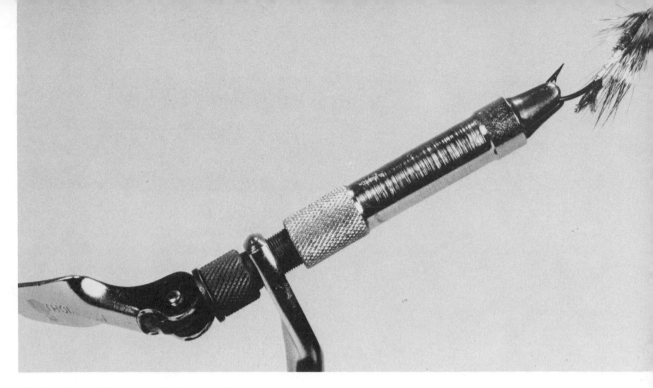

The head on a Thompson A vise turned

open and close the jaws, with a micrometer adjustment knob in the rear, three interchangeable bits that accept hooks from size 6/0 to 28, and a set ring in the middle that can be loosened so that the head can be turned. It is available in two models, Premium and Standard, both of which come with either a table clamp or solid brass stand. This tying machine is superbly machined and fitted, and like a fine split-cane salmon rod, must be tried to be appreciated.

SCISSORS

A pair of fine-pointed Iris (named after their function in eye surgery) scissors are best for the trimming of hackle fibers, floss, fine tinsel, and many other types of material that fall into the "delicate" category. Since these scissors are the ones that you will be using the most, they should be good ones. For some of the heavier work, like the cutting of quills, wire, deer hair, etc., a heavy duty pair of scissors will also be necessary. Don't buy scissors that are too short, since they won't handle nearly as well as the long ones. The two I use the most are shown in the photograph, and they are about four inches long. Naturally, good fly tying scissors should be used for that only, or they will soon be ruined or lost.

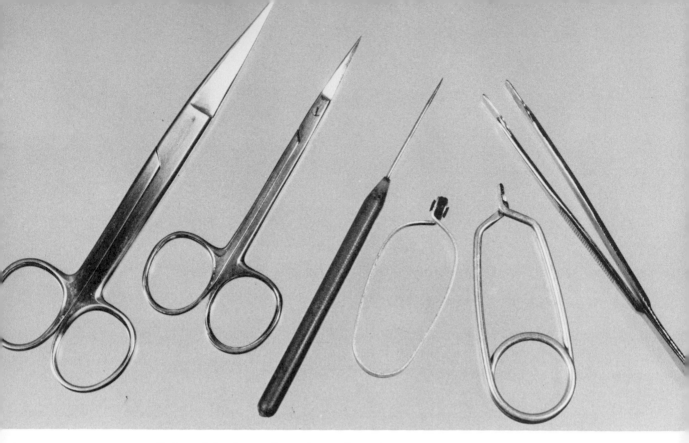

Left to right: heavy duty scissors, fine-pointed Iris scissors, dubbing needle, Thompson's rubber jaw hackle pliers, English-type hackle pliers, and flat-head tweezers.

HACKLE PLIERS

The best hackle pliers you have are your fingers, but when tying smaller flies, the hackles are often so short that they must be held with a pair of pliers. I have two types that I use most frequently: heavy English-type pliers with smooth rounded jaws, and Thompson's rubber-jawed, non-skid hackle pliers, which in my estimation are the best available.

BOBBIN

Frank Matarelli's fly tying tools have always been high on my list. He makes the finest stainless steel bobbin money can buy. The two spring-steel arms with cone-shaped balls on the ends can be adjusted to fit any spool. For tying salmon flies, it is best to have several bobbins for different colors of thread. Frank has developed a bobbin threader as a companion to the bobbin. It has a needle with a blunted end (to clean wax out of the tube) and a threader wire. They are set at opposite ends of a short piece of beadchain so that they fold up to save space.

DUBBING NEEDLE

You can easily make a dubbing needle yourself by cementing a needle into a piece of dowel. However, several on the market are relatively inexpensive. They are used for picking out fur, hackle fibers, and of course for applying cement on thread windings and fly heads.

TWEEZERS

I like the flat-head tweezers better than the pointed ones for dressing salmon flies. They enable me to pick small body feathers, such as kingfisher feathers, small hackle tips, etc., off the skins.

SURGEON'S SCALPEL

A scalpel takes the place of the razor blade as an all-purpose cutting tool, and is a great deal safer. It is particularly useful for cutting thread, splitting quill stems when making wings, and cutting pieces of skin for dyeing.

JORGENSEN WING DIVIDER

This wing divider is worth its weight in gold and was designed to separate quill strips in pairs that are exactly the same width. It's not available commercially, so you will have to make you own as follows: trim a paper clip to form the two legs; then insert it into the end of an Exacto knife handle. The long leg serves as a guide when held alongside the quill fibers, while the other is inserted in the wing quill and drawn out through the feather to separate the section. The legs can be adjusted by bending them.

SUNDRIES

Wax. For extra waxing of thread when applying fur for bodies, I use Overton's Wonder Wax, which comes in a small container in stick form. The bottom of the container can be turned to advance the stick. It is the finest I have ever used; I can highly recommend it.

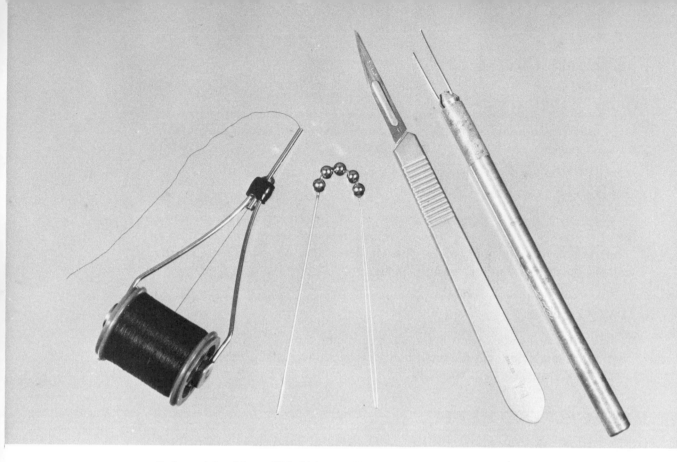

Left to right: **Matarelli bobbin, bobbin threader, surgeon's scalpel, and Jorgensen wing divider.**

Head Cement.   There are many types on the market, but nothing can beat ordinary clear nail polish with a nylon base. I use this for finishing most of the fly heads and whenever cement is needed.

Epoxy.   This adhesive is used for heads only in salmon fly dressing. It consists of a resin and a hardener that should be mixed in equal amounts. Five Minute Epoxy or Foxy Epoxy are both good and fairly fast drying, and flies with epoxy heads can usually be fished within twenty-four hours after application. *Do not use waxed thread when epoxy is to be used;* the epoxy will not set. In such cases I finish off the head with 6/0 unwaxed silk.

Lacquer.   I personally do not use lacquer except clear, on my salmon flies, but for those who do I can recommend Cellire lacquer. It comes in black, red, yellow, blue, and clear. When ordering the lacquer, get some thinner at the same time. Not all suppliers carry this, but it can be obtained from those who sell Veniard products.

HOOKS

The hooks manufactured specifically for salmon flies are easy to recognize among other fish hooks by their black-japanned finish, limerick bend, and up-turned, looped eye.

Why are salmon hooks different from the average, run-of-the-mill hooks? Well, one is tempted to say it was to make them more expensive — which they are — but there are other reasons, of course. The explanation I got when I asked was that the black japanning prevented them from rusting, and the limerick bend aided the fly in riding right-side up instead of inverting. Perhaps you can draw your own conclusions, but in any case the distinctive dark coloration is a mark of salmon flies.

The looped eye eliminates the possibility of fraying the leader (important particularly in the early days of eyed hooks when gut leaders were still used) or slipping out if the eye is not completely closed, as is often the case on ordinary hooks. Best of all, though, the extra width of the loop in front of the shank provides a convenient, flat surface on which the many wing materials can be fastened.

Both single and double hooks come in different lengths and wire diameter.

Standard Hooks. These are made of the heaviest wire and come in both single and double. Mustad single #36890 and double #3582C are 1X longer than the English hooks, which arc also available in single and double heavy wire, but regular length. Being 1X longer means that, for example, a size #2 Mustad has the same shank length as an English hook one size larger. I have always preferred the English because I think a standard salmon fly pattern is better proportioned on a regular-length hook, but that is a matter of preference.

Mustad single hooks are available in sizes 6/0 to 10; doubles from 3/0 to 12. The Mustad singles are excellent substitutes for the "Long Dee" hooks used when dressing the Dee Strip Wing and Spey flies.

Low-Water Hooks. They come in both single and double hooks also, but they are 2X long and made of finer wire. These are English hooks and are excellent for the contemporary flies which, in many cases, are dressed very sparsely. They are also used for the General Pactitioner because of the extra long shank. The singles come in sizes 6/0 through 12, and doubles in sizes 3/0 through 12.

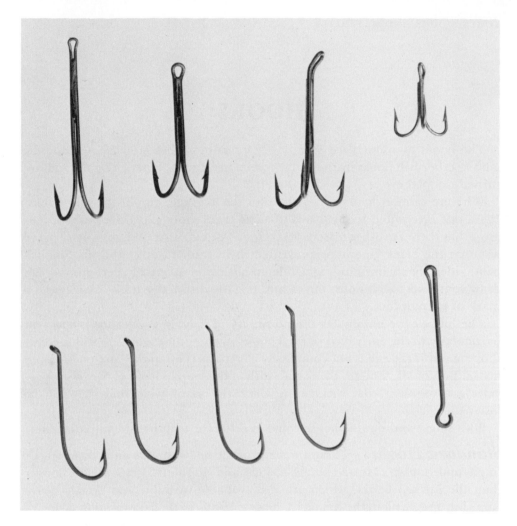

Salmon fly hooks: (top row, left to right) English double low water, English regular double, Esmund Drury treble hook, regular treble hook; (bottom row, left to right) Mustad 36890, English regular, English low water, Wilson dry fly hook, Waddington shank.

Wilson Dry Fly Hooks.

These hooks are designed specifically for dry flies and are made of very thin wire. Their hook gaps are a little wider than those of the low-water hooks. Available in sizes 4 through 10, these English hooks are of very fine quality, and some salmon anglers prefer their low-water flies dressed on these fine-wire hooks instead of the regular low-water hooks, simply because they are so light and strong.

For measuring the shank length on the various sizes of salmon fly hooks, I have included a scale that may be helpful in choosing a particular size when ordering hooks.

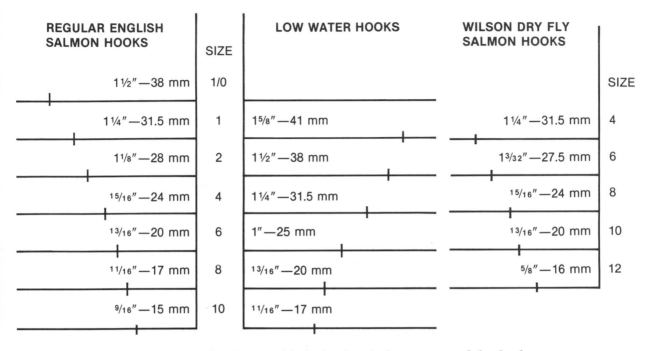

REGULAR ENGLISH SALMON HOOKS	SIZE	LOW WATER HOOKS	WILSON DRY FLY SALMON HOOKS	SIZE
1½″ —38 mm	1/0			
1¼″ —31.5 mm	1	1⅝″ —41 mm	1¼″ —31.5 mm	4
1⅛″ —28 mm	2	1½″ —38 mm	1³/₃₂″ —27.5 mm	6
¹⁵/₁₆″ —24 mm	4	1¼″ —31.5 mm	¹⁵/₁₆″ —24 mm	8
¹³/₁₆″ —20 mm	6	1″ —25 mm	¹³/₁₆″ —20 mm	10
¹¹/₁₆″ —17 mm	8	¹³/₁₆″ —20 mm	⅝″ —16 mm	12
⁹/₁₆″ —15 mm	10	¹¹/₁₆″ —17 mm		

All hook measurements are taken from outside the bend to the foremost part of the shank. When measuring hook lengths, do not include the eye.

Waddington Shanks.   These are rather unusual hooks, almost unknown in the United States. They are used in conjunction with a treble hook and are assembled for dressing of articulated flies. The shank itself has a second "eye" in the posterior end instead of a bend but is otherwise the same length as a regular salmon hook. They can be obtained in sizes 8/0 to 10.

Tubes for Tube-Flies.   These are called "slipstream" flies in England and are available from various suppliers who carry specialty items for salmon flies. The tubes that are shown in the drawing are: type A, a plastic tube with moulded ends which prevents the dressing from slipping off; type B, a long plastic tube that is stouter than type A and has a cavity in the posterior end for insertion of the hook-eye so the treble hook is always aligned; type C, an aluminum tube with a plastic lining; and type D, a brass tube with a plastic lining for heavy flies. All these tubes come in lengths of ½-inch, ¾-inch, 1 inch, 1¼-inches, 1½-inches, 1¾-inches and 2 inches.

Treble Hooks.   The regular treble hooks are used for both the Waddington shanks and the tubes. They are either bronzed or black japanned, but since the bronzed is the one that is most readily available I use those the most.

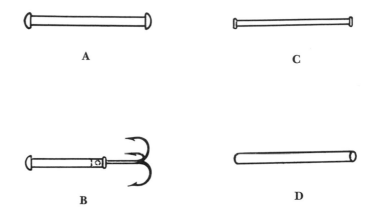

Tubes for tube flies.

Esmond Drury Treble Hooks.   These are specially designed long-shank hooks with up-turned eyes. They are japanned and come in sizes 2 to 12. Because of the up-turned eyes, they are used only for the Esmond Drury flies, which are dressed directly on the shank.

MATERIALS

If you are accustomed to tying your own trout flies, chances are that many of the materials needed for salmon fly dressing is already in your collection: thread, floss, etc. But there are certain items, particularly feathers, that will be new to you. The names of some reliable material suppliers are listed at the end of this chapter; they will be able to help you get the various items described on the following pages. Most fly tiers take great pride in their accumulation of materials and justifiably so, but to give quantity priority over quality is a great mistake. For salmon flies, especially, it is far more important to select each item carefully than it is to fill the drawers.

TYING THREAD

If you would unravel an old salmon fly, the first thing you would notice is the heavy tying thread that was used before modern technology provided us with strong, thin nylon threads. These new threads are indeed a blessing to the salmon fly dresser.

I prefer Herb Howard's 6/0 pre-waxed tying thread for most of my work. It is as strong as 3/0 silk, but is much thinner. The colors that you will need for salmon flies are black, white, red, yellow, green, and orange. If epoxy is used on the head of a finished fly, it is best to finish it off with 6/0 silk. The wax in the other thread will not permit epoxy to dry properly.

Heavier threads in sizes B, 2/0, and 3/0 silk or nylon will be needed if you make deer-hair bodies for the Irresistible and McDougal dry flies and also for the Muddler head.

FLOSS

Floss is a flat, ribbonlike material, either silk or rayon, and comes in heavy, single-strand stock or in four-strand spools. It must always be untwisted before it is wound, or it will tie unevenly. It is used for bodies and tags on many salmon flies; the most important colors are yellow, lemon yellow, golden yellow, black, orange, red, lilac, green, hot orange, and light blue. Many of these colors are also available in fluorescent stock, which is often used for tags on the contemporary hair-wing patterns, like the Butt's and Roger's Fancy.

WOOL

Wool is used for whole bodies, butts, and heads. The best I have found is ordinary crewel wool used for embroidery. A single strand can be separated and wound as a body, or it can be shredded and dubbed on the tying thread when used for butts and heads on flies like the Silver Doctor and Black Doctor. The important colors are black, red, bright green, hot orange, brown, orange, lemon yellow, and olive green.

CHENILLE

This is the same material used for trout flies; it looks very much like a pipe cleaner, but the fuzzy material is spun on a center core of silk. It is not used very much in salmon fly dressing, except on flies by Martinez of Spain, and only in very fine yellow and medium bright green and insect green.

TINSEL

The French make the best tinsel in the world, but unfortunately it is somewhat scarce today. Most of what is available comes from India and other countries; these products are very acceptable if the French is not available. The following tinsels are needed in both gold and silver.

Oval.   Oval tinsel is a very narrow, flat tinsel that is wound over a cotton core and flattened. It is used mostly for tags and ribbing, but sometimes whole bodies or parts of them are made by winding it tightly over the entire shank. It comes in very fine, fine, medium, and wide.

Round.   This tinsel is made the same way as the oval tinsel but is not flattened. In England the round tinsel is often referred to as "twist" and is often called for in some of the more elaborate flies. You will need fine and medium sizes for ordinary work.

Lace.   A cord is formed by winding several strands of round tinsel (twist) together, usually three. If you are lucky enough to get a spool of readymade lace, it is probably best to keep it in a safe, as it is very rare, at least in America. I have always made my own by twisting three strands of fine round tinsel together, or I have simply left it out of the pattern.

Wire.   This is not really a tinsel, but simply a very fine wire used as tags on some flies.

Flat.   There are two types of flat tinsel: the regular, smooth, ribbonlike stock; and the embossed variety. Both types are available in narrow, medium, and wide. It is used for making solid silver or gold bodies and for tags and ribbing on some salmon flies. A number of brands of flat mylar tinsels are now available.

Mylar.   The flat, synthetic mylar tinsels are both easier to work with than metal tinsel, and do not tarnish. Some suppliers have brands that are silver on one side and gold on the other. Braided mylar tubing in both silver and gold is used for tube flies and is applied in a manner explained in the chapter dealing with tube flies.

Copper.   This type of tinsel is used least in salmon fly dressing, but one should have some fine and medium copper wire and medium flat copper tinsel. If the supplier does not stock the copper, I am sure he can order it for you.

LATEX

This high grade rubber material comes in small 5x5-inch sheets and is available from most suppliers. I use it for wingcases on the salmon fur nymphs. It should be heavy duty latex since it's mostly used for large nymphs. One can use a small paper cutter or a scalpel and ruler to cut it into strips. Or simply trim out the small segments with your heavy duty scissors.

FUR

Seal.   Seal's fur is the most widely used material for salmon fly bodies. It's a very coarse and translucent fur that is sometimes difficult to dub on the tying thread. I often apply some extra wax on the thread for better adherence.

Because of import restrictions and the fact that baby seals are now on the endangered species list, this important material is difficult to obtain. When faced with a shortage some years ago, I developed a very fine synthetic substitute called Seal-Ex. It has a very high translucency and dubs easier than the real fur. Seal-Ex is available from your supplier in sets of eighteen colors or by single colors in small tubes. Whichever you use, the colors you will need for salmon fly bodies are black, red, yellow, yellowish orange, hot orange, fiery brown, claret, Green Highlander green, purple, and light blue.

Fur for Dry Flies.   The underfur from the red and gray fox provides the shades of cream and gray that are needed for the dry flies I have included in this book. If a darker gray is needed, I suggest the underfur from a muskrat. A very dark underfur can be obtained from the woodchuck.

Rabbit Fur.   This type of fur is used for spinning the leg and thorax (front portion on the nymph) part of the salmon fur nymph. Since these nymphs generally have some markings on their legs, I find that the well-marked guardhair on the back of a brown rabbit is best suited for the nymphs in this book. It can be obtained in natural tannish gray to medium brown and can be dyed in any other color you may need.

FEATHERS

Most fly tiers who are just learning to dress their own salmon flies have never seen the exotic feathers like toucan, Indian crow, macaw, and blue chatterer that often are called for in traditional salmon fly patterns. For the rest of us, well—they are but a memory. We have, however, somehow managed to find feathers that can be dyed for good substitutes, or have simply left out those that seem nonessential. The speckled bustard, florican bustard and peacock wing quills are almost nonexistent today. The wild turkey has mottled tails and wing quills in various shades that make excellent substitutes for these feathers. Moreover, this state of affairs need not be taken overly seriously in dressing flies for fishing. Invention and improvisation are essential elements of flytying, and they apply equally to the most revered traditional salmon patterns. For a Jock Scott wing, for example, which calls for speckled and florican bustard in the original pattern, I "marry" the yellow, scarlet and blue fibers, and then merely marry a broad strip of brown-mottled turkey tail of medium shade to the upper edge of those. This arrangement works well—the fish don't seem to notice the difference! For exhibit flies that are to be framed, I use the few real McCoys I have saved for just such occasions.

The description of the various feathers that follow, their substitutes, and the methods of dyeing those that need to be is meant to be a guide, not an absolute solution. Perhaps you will find other feathers that make better replacements for the originals. If so, by all means use them. It may be helpful to refer to the color plate as you read down the list, to become familiar with the qualities of these exotic feathers.

Amherst Pheasant.   The tail has black and white (silver) markings and the neck feathers (tippets) are white with two black bars. They are used for wings on the popular Lady Amherst fly, and strands of tippet are used for tails on several other popular flies.

Bustard (Speckled).   These wing quills are no longer available, but the oak-brown-mottled turkey tails or secondary wing feathers are excellent substitutes. A few fibers from these quills are found in the married wings on most of the fully dressed salmon flies.

Bustard (Florican).   Like the speckled Bustard, these quills are all but impossible to come by, although you may occasionally be offered a small supply from a friendly material dealer. They have rather wide black and buff (pale tan) stripes and can be substituted by dyeing a dark gray and white turkey wing feather tan.

Cock of the Rock.   This bright orange feather is substituted with dyed webby saddle or hen neck hackle. The feathers are used for the wing on the Orange Parson. For dyeing instructions see "Dyes and Dyeing" later in this chapter.

Crow (Black).   The wing quills from this bird are as black as you would ever want. They are used for wings on the Sweep and the Night Hawk.

Golden Pheasant.   This bird is the most important supplier of feathers for salmon flies, and almost every feather is used in one pattern or another. The tail is brown with black markings and is used in many salmon fly wings. The golden yellow crest is used as a "topping" on most flies, and the neck feathers are used in whole feather wings, like the Orange Parson and the Ranger series. Strands from the tippet are also used for underwings and in tails for many flies. The golden pheasant also supplies the reddish orange flank and breast feathers used on the General Practitioner and Shrimp flies.

Goose.   The shoulder feathers (nashurias) from the goose are substitutes for swan, which can no longer be obtained. The small ones are about four inches and the large ones about six to seven inches long. Both of these are needed so that you can dress both small and large flies. Since they usually have the quill in the middle of the feather, you can use one side for the left wing and the other side for the right. Dyed black, yellow, red, orange, green, and blue, these are the feathers from which strands are taken and married to form a part of almost all wings on fully dressed salmon flies. When buying them, make sure they are shoulder feathers. Often the supplier will send you wing quills, which are absolutely useless for married wings.

Guinea Fowl.   The tail and wing quills are used for sides and wings, and the breast and flank feathers are used as throat hackle on many flies. They come in two different marking patterns: black with white spots, or gray speckled, both feathers being found on the same bird. The body feathers are often dyed silver doctor blue for use as a substitute for blue jay, which is hard to get and difficult to use.

Hen Pheasant.   The tan- and buff-mottled tail and wing quills are used for simple strip wings on small flies like the March Brown.

Heron.   The gray breast feathers and black crest feathers are highly sought after for hackle on flies like the Grey Heron and the Akroyd. They cannot be obtained regularly in America because all heron are on the endangered species list. They can be substituted by dyeing the long, fibered rump feathers from a common ringneck pheasant either gray or black. In many instances it is not even necessary to dye them; their natural, light brownish gray shade will do nicely for fishing. The hen (chicken) also has some soft tail and rump feathers that make excellent heron substitutes. They can be obtained in natural black or gray.

Indian Crow.   The scarlet breast feathers are called for in tails, cheeks, and veilings on many of the fancier flies. Like so many other feathers, Indian crow is no longer available. The best substitutes I have found are small, soft hen neck hackles, buff-colored body feathers from a hen pheasant, or the white feathers around the neck of a common ringneck pheasant. All these feathers can be dyed scarlet. (See dyeing intructions later in this chapter.)

Patterns

LEFT ROW
top to bottom

Orange Parson
Jock Scott
Blue Charm
Thunder and Lightning

RIGHT ROW
top to bottom

Silver Ranger
Black Doctor
Crossfield
Silver Blue (Low Water)

LEFT ROW
top to bottom

Grey Heron
Hairy Mary Tube Fly
General Practitioner
Jungle Hornet
Shrimp Fly

RIGHT ROW
top to bottom

Waddington Thunder and
    Lightning
Akroyd (White Winged)
Krabla Fly
Tippet Grub
Silver Doctor (Drury Treble
    Hook)

Patterns

LEFT ROW
top to bottom

Rusty Rat
Salmon Fur Nymph
Soldier Palmer (Dry Fly)
Royal Wulff (Dry Fly)

RIGHT ROW
top to bottom

Blue Rat
Bomber (Dry Fly)
Skater (Dry Fly)
Grizzly Wulff (Dry Fly)

Peacock (Wing).   Like the bustards, these quills are hard to get, and the gray-mottled turkey tail is used as a substitute. A few fibers are used for some patterns and married with others to form the wing.

Peacock Herl.   The peacock "eyed" tail provides the tier with some long herls sitting on each side of the long quill stem. They are bronze green and used for bodies on several flies, including the well-known Rusty and Blue Rats.

Peacock Sword.   Only the tip portion with the slightly curved herls are used. They sit on one side of the quill stem and are used in wings and tails of several flies, including the Rusty Rat, Jock Scott, and Roger's Fancy.

Pintail.   Pintail flank feathers are pale gray with heavy black stripes and are often mistaken for either mallard or teal. They are used for sides and throats. Only a few material houses carry the feathers in the United States and so one is obliged to use mallard or teal as a substitute.

Ringneck Cock Pheasant.   This bird offers many excellent feathers for fly tying, but for salmon flies we are concerned only with the long center tails. The fibers are very strong, varying in shade from tan to brown and purple, and they can be dyed to darker colors for tails on salmon nymph patterns.

Spey Hackle.   Spey hackle is used for flies bearing the name "Spey flies." They sit on the side of the tail on roosters, but are not available in the United States. Large, webby hackles and hen or rooster rump feathers in gray and black make acceptable substitutes.

Swan.   See "Goose."

Teal.   Teal flank and body feathers are white with heavy black bars which make them very effective for all kinds of flies. In some cases they are used for entire wings, as on the Crossfield, and on others for sides or hackle in conjunction with other feathers. If they are used as hackle, it is best to strip one side completely off the stem, or tie them on in bunches.

Toucan.   This bird's golden orange breast feathers, once used for tails and veilings, are not available any more, and a substitute is needed. I use the white feathers from the collar of a ringneck pheasant, or small hen neck feather, which I have dyed golden orange. You need only one of these feathers for each veiling, whereas you need four to six natural feathers if you still have some. (See dyeing instructions later in the chapter.)

Turkey.   Together with the golden pheasant, the wild turkey is the most important bird for the salmon fly dresser. It literally supplies all the natural quills needed for wings. The tails come in many shades and several lengths.

The longest of these comes in medium or dark brown mottled and has the white tip strips that are used as an underwing in the Jock Scott, Dusty Miller, and many others. For smaller flies I also use the smallest white-tipped rump feathers. These are metallic black with tannish white tips. The tails also come in cinnamon for wings on such flies as the Akroyd, and in a pale tan or gray mottled shade that is substituted for peacock wing. While these tails are twelve inches or longer, there is a smaller one that is about six to seven inches long and comes in many shades. I prefer them over the others because they are easier to marry with the dyed goose strips, and they also make better strip wings for flies like the Blue Charm.

The secondary wing feathers are oak brown mottled and brown mottled; they are used for wings and are good substitutes for both peacock and speckled bustard. It is interesting to collect these feathers and find so many different shades—all of which can be used at one time or another.

Woodduck (Also Called Summer Duck or Mandarin).   For dressing salmon flies, you need get only the flank feathers with the black bars. They are used as sides or in tails on many of the better-known flies. Unfortunately, they will often have to be left out because they are hard to get at times. If you are offered some, don't hesitate to take them, even at a rather high cost, because they have no substitute.

HACKLE FOR WET FLIES

There are three styles of hackle application you can use on salmon wet flies: the hackle collar, which is wound in front after the wing is tied in; the throat hackle sitting underneath the shank; and the palmer body hackle. In some instances the hackle collar, or the throat, is combined with the body hackle on the same fly; but the hackles you use should be different in texture. A tendency to use hackle that is too stiff, almost dry fly quality, badly hinders the "breathing" action when fished. The following hackles are the ones I prefer. They may differ considerably from those preferred by others, but I have found that they work best for me.

Hackle for Throat and Collar.   Since I like the hackle to breathe and be as alive looking as possible, I use either third-grade rooster hackle or good grade hen neck hackle. Both of these feathers are rather webby in texture, and I also use the webby portions of saddle hackles, as long as they are soft. It is best to get whole necks and saddles for good selection in the following colors: black, red, yellow, hot orange, lemon yellow, olive brown, purple, magenta, claret, light claret, green highlander, kingfisher blue (silver doctor),

and deep blue. In addition to the dyed colors, you will need grizzly (plymouth rock), which is a natural dark gray or black feather with white barring.

Bird Hackle.   The body and flank feathers from several specific birds are often used for dressing the throat and for hackle collars. The most important ones are taken from guinea fowl, mallard, teal, golden pheasant, vulturine, heron, and partridge. The latter are the gray and pale-brown-mottled back and breast feathers that have a brownish bar at the tip section, often used for legs in nymph patterns like the March Brown. The other feathers have been described previously under feathers used for wings. These feathers may occasionally cause some trouble when being wound, in which case I suggest that you strip off one side. Since most hackles are wound in a clockwise direction, it is important that the correct side be stripped off. To determine which side to strip, place the feather on the table with the good side up and the tip portion pointing upward. If the feather is to be tied in by the butt, you strip off the fibers from the right side of the quill stem. If it is to be tied in by the tip, the left side is stripped off.

Hackle for Bodies.   A great many flies have a palmered hackle over the body in addition to the throat or collar hackle. These should be of a considerably better quality than those mentioned before. I like saddle hackles and poor grade dry fly hackles for this type of work. In addition to the colors mentioned earlier, you will need a natural badger, which is a creamy white hackle with a black center stripe. It is used in its natural state for flies like the Silver Grey and the Lady Amherst. This hackle is also dyed yellow for body hackle on the Durham Ranger. Finally, you will need furnace, coachman brown (fiery brown), and cock-y-bondhu. The furnace is a brown shade with a black center stripe, and the cock-y-bondhu is very similar—the only difference being a black list at the tip of the individual fibers. It is possible that in time you will need other shades and types of hackle, for which the supplier's catalogues can give you a good description.

HACKLE FOR DRY FLIES

While low grade hackle will suffice for the dressing of wet flies, the opposite is the case for dry flies. For them I use the very best rooster neck and saddle hackle I can obtain. To be able to dress the dry flies included in this book you will need the following hackles: grizzly, coachman brown, ginger, blue dun, furnace, and badger. It is always best to purchase whole necks and saddle patches to have a good variety from which to select.

HAIR

Almost any hair that is not too stiff can be used for wings on salmon flies. I prefer the natural shades whenever they are available, but there is also a great need for dyed hair, particularly for mixing into the wings on the hair-wing versions of the old classics.

Bear.   The hair from both the brown and black bear is useful in many patterns. It varies a great deal in stiffness, depending on the part of the bear from which it is taken. As a whole it can only be classified as a coarse hair; most bear is not suitable for small flies.

Bucktail.   Both the white and natural brown hair is used and is found on the same tail. The white can be dyed any color for use in mixed-hair wings and tails and feelers and on some of the shrimp flies. The natural brown is used in any wing that requires a natural medium shade of fairly coarse hair and, of course, for wings on many of the dry flies.

Calf Tail.   The hair is natural white, except for the tip portion, which can provide you with some natural brown or black hair. It is fairly curly and crinkled but can be straightened by rolling the hair bunch between your fingers. Like the bucktail, it can be dyed any color. The white hair is highly sought after for wings on such dry flies as the Royal Wulff and the White Wulff.

Deer Body Hair.   This is the grayish brown and white hollow hair used for such flies as the Muddler, Irresistible, Bomber, and other important flies that require a trimmed deer-hair body. While it is normally used in its natural color, it can be dyed any color you wish.

Fitchtail.   The guardhair on the tip section of these small tails is very soft and shiny. It ranges in color from dark brown to black. The rest of the tail is creamy white, but it can be dyed any shade. Due to the shortness of the hair, it is not suitable for flies larger than size 4.

Gray Fox.   The guardhairs on the back of the gray fox are very important for the Rat patterns and the Roger's Fancy. The hair is grayish black with a distinct white bar. The underfur is gray and should be saved for dry fly bodies.

Polar Bear.   Here is a very fine, translucent hair that can be dyed any color. I prefer hair that is about two inches long and dyed black, red, yellow, green highlander green, orange, and blue. This is the best hair for mixing into multicolored hair wings but since it is fairly coarse hair, I don't favor it for whole wings.

Squirrel Tail (Gray).   The hair is speckled with a black bar and white tip. It is often used for entire wings and supporting underwings. Like other hair, it can be dyed any color.

Squirrel Tail (Red Fox).   The hair on these tails is reddish brown with black bars. Like the gray squirrel, it is used for wings on several of the important hair-wing flies.

Squirrel Tail (Eastern Pine).   These tails have the same general shade as the red fox squirrel, but they are much smaller — four to six inches. The soft, short hair is used for the Blue Charm hair wing and other important flies. Due to the shortness of the hair, it is usable only for small flies up to size 2.

Squirrel Tail (Black).   Natural black squirrel tail is not easy to get, but occasionally it is offered for sale by private individuals. Do not turn it down, even if the price seems high. Black squirrel tails are the same size as gray squirrel and can provide some fine natural hair wings.

Woodchuck (Groundhog).   The guardhairs are used as substitutes for both gray fox and eastern pine squirrel, and a woodchuck wing on a Blue Charm is very nice indeed. The underfur is a dark, grayish black shade that can be used for dry fly bodies. Some skins have some brown guardhairs on the sides that can also be used for wings and tails on dry flies.

DYES AND DYEING

Most of the material you will need can be obtained from your supplier already dyed to the specifications outlined in the material lists for the various patterns. But there is a great satisfaction in being able to dye your own material so that you can precisely control the shades or special colors you may need.

Dyeing for personal use is fairly simple: All you need are two stainless steel saucepans: one small one that will hold a cup of water when half full, and a second one somewhat larger that will hold two to four cups. The diameter of the larger should be such that a whole neck will fit without being too crammed. The only other items you will need are a stick or spoon to stir with, a set of measuring spoons, and a strainer. You can make the strainer yourself by punching a bunch of holes in an aluminum cakepan with a one-sixteenth-inch nail.

The critical part of dyeing is the cleaning of the material and the quality of the dyestuff you are using. I cannot stress strongly enough that *materials must be thoroughly cleaned* in good, strong soap suds, particularly feathers from waterfowl. I often soak hair and feather for several hours and rub them with my fingers before rinsing them under hot running water. Until you get some experience in dyeing, I suggest that you dye small amounts so that a whole bunch of material is not ruined in experimenting.

The best dyestuff for fly tying material that I have used comes from E. Veniard in England. (Names and addresses of material suppliers are listed at the end of this chapter.) Each dye package comes with complete instructions, and the proportions of water and dyestuff indicated. It is suggested that you bring a quart of water to a boil in the larger saucepan, then stir a quarter teaspoon of dye into it and dissolve the powder thoroughly. Since the feathers themselves must not boil, when you're ready to dye, add a little cold water to bring the dyebath below the boiling point. Place the material in the dyebath and add a tablespoon of white vinegar to fix the color. Keep the burner on very low so that it is always just below the boiling point. Keep stirring and moving the material so the dye has a chance to penetrate all the fibers. Bear in mind that the materials are always much darker when wet, so you will have to check the color carefully. You can get a pretty accurate idea of the shade you will end up with by watching the color on the quill stems of the feathers. Some dyes take very fast, but others, notably black, brown, and red, must sit longer, sometimes hours, before they are satisfactory. When the material is thoroughly dyed to the shade you need, remove it from the bath and rinse it in lukewarm water until the water running off the material is completely clear. Now press the material between newspaper pages and allow to dry.

When you are dyeing small amounts of material (for example the small substitute toucan and Indian crow feathers), you can use half the prescribed amount of water and dye powder. Most dyes are straight as they come, but there are times when a special shade requires mixing a little of this and a little of that. Measuring spoons usually come no smaller than $1/8$ teaspoon, but sometimes a $1/16$ or $1/32$ teaspoon is needed. To measure these amounts I use a simple trick I learned from Lefty Kreh: take $1/8$ of a drawn teaspoon of dye and empty it onto a piece of glass. Spread it very thinly to the form of a coin with a knife and divide it into as many equal sections as you wish — just like cutting a layer cake.

Listed below are the dyes and formulas I have found useful for the material I dye most often:

GOOSE QUILLS

Yellow	Veniards yellow
Red	Veniards red or scarlet
Blue	Veniards kingfisher

GOOSE QUILLS	Green	Veniards green highlander
	Orange	Veniards orange
INDIAN CROW		Veniards, 1 part red, 1 part hot orange
BLUE CHATTERER		Veniards kingfisher
TOUCAN		Veniards light orange, or Veniards yellow with just a sprinkle of hot orange added
COCK OF THE ROCK		Veniards, 1 part yellow, ½ part hot orange. The feather is a deep, bright orange.
SILVER DOCTOR BLUE		Veniards kingfisher

MATERIAL SUPPLIERS

Hunter Fly Shop
Valley View Lane
New Boston, NH 03070

Jack's Tackle
301 Bridge Street
Phoenixville, PA 19460

Hackle and Tackle
Central Square, NY 13036

E. Veniard, Ltd
138 Northwood Road
Thornton Heath
Surrey, England

The Rivergate
Route 9—Box 275
Cold Spring, NY 10516

Fly Dressing
Box 2003
561 02 Huskvarna
Sweden

Jock Scott
Postbox 1245
8210 Aarhus V.
Denmark

EM-TE Flugbindingsmaterial
Box 70
S 310 58 Vessigebro
Sweden

Fly Fishermans Bookcase
3890 Stewart Road
Eugene, OR 97402

Dick Surette Fly Fishing Shop
Rt. 16, Box 686
North Conway, NH 03860

2

Character and Style

Fishing with any type of flies other than those for salmon, there are a number of things the angler can do to adapt them to existing conditions. For example, in trout fishing the fish are anticipating a certain species of insect to appear on the stream at a specific time and are waiting to feed on them. The angler who prefers to fish with a nymph will soon discover at which level the fish are taking the active natural. Sometimes he will fish his nymph on or near the bottom and it will require additional weight to get it down, while he at other times will fish it unweighted right in the surface film, often dressed with a dry fly floatant of some sort. The trout angler anticipates such conditions and usually carries both weighted and unweighted nymphs in the fly box.

In salmon fishing, however, it's quite different. In the first place, salmon are not supposed to be feeding at all when they return on a spawning run to their native river. Secondly, the flies that are used, with a few exceptions, are not supposed to imitate anything in particular. Thirdly, it is considered bad manners if you wish, and on some rivers, even unlawful to weight your flies.

This leaves the salmon angler with a very difficult problem. He must be able to regulate his flies so that they can be fished at a certain depth, which at any given moment may change. Carrying just flies in dark, light and bright shades is not valid and will not guarantee success. Therefore, he must have flies within each group that are dressed to be fished deep or shallow, whichever the case may be, and dressed without adding any lead weight and without changing the all-important "character" and "style" of the flies.

It is not an easy task to thoroughly explain the character and style of a salmon fly in anything less than a book unto itself. I will leave that field to angling historians who are better qualified. Here I will simply discuss the obvious differences between the various patterns and how these differences affect the angler's and the fly dresser's efforts to produce a fly that is useful for prevailing fishing conditions, and yet remain within the framework of traditional salmon fly character and style.

While the distinctive character and style of salmon flies seems obvious to the eye (especially to the trout fly tier's eye), these terms acquire their own meaning in the context of actually dressing the flies. The difference between the two terms as they apply to salmon flies is a rather broad one, and one that perhaps best be explained by illustration.

The four flies in the photograph are typical examples of the different characters which exist among salmon flies with particular reference to their shape and form. The fully dressed feather wing, the hair wings, the Spey flies, and the more imitative shrimp pattern—each of these examples of salmon fly character represents a different approach to the actual dressing, and strategically speaking, to the fishing. After learning the basic steps in dressing, one

Character differences among salmon flies. *Top left*, the Jock Scott, a fully dressed feather wing; *lower left*, the Rusty Rat, a hair wing; *top right*, the Gray Heron, a Spey fly; *lower right*, the Shrimp fly, an imitative pattern.

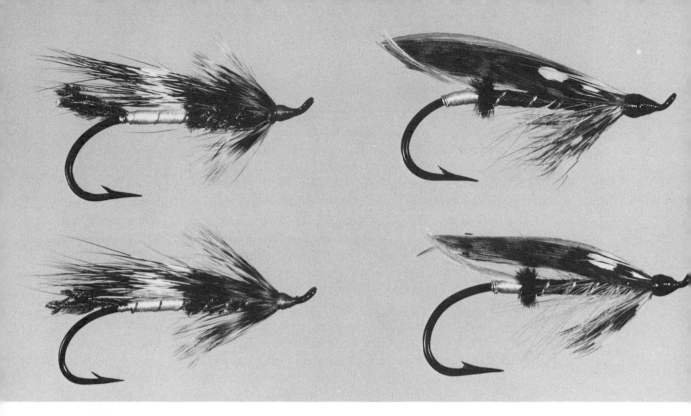

Style differences among salmon flies. *Left,* **Rusty Rat hair wings;** *right,* **fully dressed Thunder and Lightnings.**

must carefully study the methods for dressing the individual group, and others with a character all their own, so that the same patterns can actually take on this character, depending on how it is tied.

While the matter of character is primarily of concern to the fly dresser, style directly affects the angler as well in the sense that this particular aspect of the salmon fly is determined by the amount of dressing and the type of hook on which it is applied. This, in turn, will regulate the sink rate of the fly, which is of great importance to the serious salmon angler.

In the next photograph are four other flies, which in this case illustrate style and how it can be changed. The two flies on the left are Rusty Rat hair wings, dressed alike with the same amount of material applied. The top one is dressed on a heavier hook than the other one. The intention is that the one with the heavier hook is made to sink deeper a little faster than the other. (See chapter 1 for specifications.) The second method of regulating style and sink rate is illustrated by the two flies to the right in the same photograph. Both are dressed on identical hooks, and both are fully dressed Thunder & Lightnings. As it clearly illustrates, one fly is larger than the other—the idea being that the smaller fly will sink faster because there is less resistance from the smaller amount of material. The size difference is accomplished by positioning the tag on the smaller fly so that it starts directly above the point of the hook, and then changing the proportions accordingly.

In angling language, the flies in the first method of regulating style and sink rate are referred to as being dressed "heavy" or "light." In the second method they are referred to as being dressed "full" or "sparse." There is a third method, the "low-water style," that is fully explained in a chapter of its own.

But in order to approach tying salmon flies in any of these styles, and before one can make any intelligent changes in the character of the fly, one must become thoroughly familiar with the basic anatomical parts and normal proportions, which in the case of salmon flies is more rigid than for any other type of artificial fly. This is partly because the classic patterns are a product of a long tradition that is at the heart of fishing for salmon, a tradition which evolved in an era when "character and style" mattered a great deal in all aspects of life. Dressing salmon flies is one of the few expressions of those qualities we have left to us today. And it is not without its practicalities on the river, as the experienced salmon angler will attest. The mysteries of salmon fishing—why a mature, thirty-pound fish on an instinctual migration to its home spawning grounds should strike at a bright flash of feathers in the current—these are mysteries that most anglers, in their heart of hearts, want to preserve.

To participate in the deep traditions of salmon fly dressing, one must begin at the beginning: the anatomical parts of a salmon fly.

ANATOMY AND PROPORTIONS

1. Hook Bend.   The rear-most portion of the hook; often used as a point of reference for gauging the length of wings and other materials.

2. Hook Point.   Like the hook bend, a convenient point of reference, at least for the fly dresser. It is often referred to during the tying instructions as well as in material lists for various patterns.

3. Point of Barb.   The third point of reference used in gauging the overall proportions of the various materials.

4. Hook Gap.   A measurement often used during the tying instructions and mentioned in dressings for determining the tail and hackle length, wing width, etc.

5. Hook Eye.   The forward-most part of the hook, starting at the point where it is bent upward.

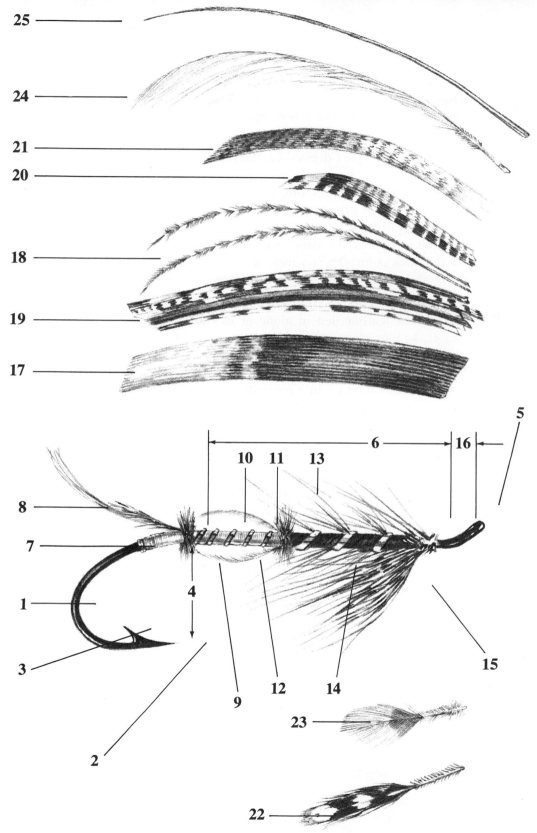

Anatomical parts of a Jock Scott (Drawing by Bill Elliott).

6. Hook Shank. The portion of the hook on which the body is dressed. It reaches from where the eye is bent upward to a place directly above the hook point.

7. Tag. The first part dressed on the hook, and consists of flat, embossed, round, or oval tinsel or wire, in gold, silver, or copper. Each of the tinsels and wires can be used in combination with floss, except the flat variety, which will not keep the floss in place. A typical tag consists of two or three turns of fine oval tinsel applied directly above the hook barb, followed by a floss segment starting close against the tinsel segment and extending forward to a point above the hook point. The position of the tag may be changed, in which case the style and overall proportions of the fly will be affected.

8. Tail. The tail on old established patterns invariably consisted of a golden pheasant crest feather tied in alone or in combination with tippet strands, Indian crow, blue chatterer or blue kingfisher, fibers from teal flank, black-barred woodduck, plain hackle fibers dyed in various colors, and many other combinations. The length of the tail is usually one-and-a-half hook gaps, unless otherwise called for in a particular dressing, or unless the tag is located in any other position than the one described in point 7 dealing with the tag. (Also see chapter 2 dealing with character and style, and chapter 5 dealing with low-water flies.) When a second material is used in the tail, it should be half as long as the tail unless otherwise called for in the dressing. On contemporary flies, such as hair-wing patterns, tiers often deviate from tradition by using hair, hackle fibers, floss, or peacock as tails. The length of such tails should be the same as those of golden pheasant crest or as described in the tying instructions or material lists.

9. Butt. Located directly in front of the tag, the butt is wound after the tail is tied in. Sometimes several butts of different colors and materials are used on the body, for example three butts with a contrasting color in the middle, in which case they are often referred to as joints. They are made of either ostrich herl, peacock herl, wool, or Seal-Ex dubbing in a variety of colors; black, red, and green are the most common.

10. Body. Bodies can be dressed with many different types of material, either alone or in combination with one another. The most commonly used are flat, embossed, or oval tinsel in silver and gold, and floss, seal's fur or Seal-Ex dubbing, wool, chenille, and peacock herl in a variety of colors listed in chapter 1.

11. Ribbing. The ribbing on most salmon flies is either oval or flat silver or gold tinsel. On continuous bodies not broken up by butts, the ribbing is spiraled on the entire length, taking the traditional five turns. (See explanation in chapter 3 under "Tying in the Body and Ribbing.") On bodies that are broken up by butts, the tinsel is wound separately on each section, taking from two to five turns depending on the size of the body portion. The size or width of the ribbing tinsel is chosen to suit the size fly being dressed, and one can get a fairly good idea of ribbing styles by studying the proportions of the flies that are dealt with in the tying instructions.

It is interesting to note that, by a long tradition, there are only five turns of ribbing on a salmon fly body, which may seem irrelevant since no one has ever proven that a salmon can count. But perhaps there is one reason that makes sense: Many of the fully dressed classic salmon flies are dressed with a hackle palmered over the body from the second turn of the tinsel, and it is wound in such a manner that each turn of hackle is placed tight behind each turn of tinsel. If there were more than five turns of tinsel, the hackle would be too dense and thus adversely affect the performance of the fly.

12. Veilings.   Indian crow or toucan breast feathers incorporated into bodies that are broken up in one or more segments. Sometimes floss is also used for veilings, such as in the Rusty Rat and Blue Rat hair wings. The veilings are tied in flat above and below on certain body portions, as called for in the dressing.

13. Joint (Butt).   Often used to break the body up into two or more segments. It is most often made of ostrich herl, but peacock herl wool, seal's fur, and Seal-Ex dubbing is often called for.

14. Hackle.   The hackle on salmon wet flies means a hackle palmered over the body and applied closely behind the tinsel ribbing to protect it from the fish's teeth. (Also see Throat.) Therefore, bodies with a palmered hackle should always be ribbed with oval or round tinsel. If flat tinsel is used—and it sometimes is—it must be in conjunction with either oval or round tinsel applied so it follows tight against and behind the flat, which is wound on first. Soft neck or saddle hackles, either natural or dyed in any color, can be used for ribbing hackle, provided it has a good translucency. Choose the hackle so the fibers on the first turn in the rear are about one hook gap in length.

15. Throat.   Often referred to as the beard. It sits in front under the shank. The feathers I prefer to use are rather soft and webby saddle hackle with some fill to them. Body hackles from guinea fowl, teal, and others are also used, either natural or dyed. If a fly has a body hackle, the throat is applied so it blends smoothly without any gap between them. While the throat in most cases is set under the shank, there are some hair-wing and simple strip-wing patterns where it is wound as a collar in front, in which case it's referred to as a hackle. The throat should be slightly longer than the front of the body hackle, or one and one-half hook gaps unless otherwise indicated in the dressing.

16. Head Space.   The space in front of the body between the eye and the windings that fasten the throat and wing. The butt ends from those materials must be trimmed short so they do not pass beyond the allotted space. Practice will teach you how to properly gauge the room needed for the short, stubby head.

17. Underwing.   Used as support for the main wing, which is attached over it. They can be a variety of different materials: strips of white-tipped turkey, jungle cock feathers, whole tippets, tippet in strands, golden pheasant tail and hackles, each used alone or in combination with one another. These feathers are nearly always set back-to-back on top of the hook shank.

18. Peacock Sword.   Sometimes used in combination with the rest of the wing material; peacock herl is also used in some patterns for effect.

19. Main Wing.   Can be a broad strip of many sorts of tail, wing, or body feather, or strands of natural or dyed feathers married to form a wing, in which case it is assembled in the order written in the material list for a particular pattern, starting from the lower edge. The width of the strip should be about half a hook gap and reach to just inside the tail unless otherwise indicated in the dressing.

20. Outer Wing.   Sitting on the outside of the main wing, usually in the middle, and reaching to above the butt. Broad strips of teal or black-barred woodduck are used, either alone or by marrying several strands of each. The width of the strips alone or combined is about half the width of the main wing.

21. Upper Wing Edge.   Often called the "roof," the upper wing edge envelopes the upper perimeter of the wing and is tied in last. It is normally half the width of the outer wing unless otherwise specified and reaches to the end of the main wing. Most commonly used are strips of brown mallard shoulder feather or, as it is often called, bronze mallard.

22. Side.   Located on the outside of the outer wing or, in absence of the outer wing, outside of the main wing. Jungle cock is most widely used, but broad strips of teal, black-barred woodduck, and plain hackles natural or dyed may be used. Jungle cock feathers should usually be one-third to half a wing length, and other feathers are most often longer or as specified in the particular dressing.

23. Cheek.   Either Indian crow or blue chatterer are used. Cheeks sit on the outside of the sides and should be about a half to one hook gap in length unless otherwise called for in the dressing.

24. Topping.   A golden pheasant crest feather tied in over the finished wing, following the upper perimeter, with the tip reaching to join exactly with the tip of the tail.

25. Horns.   Two single strands of macaw tail, either reddish orange or red, and blue and yellow. They are tied in above or in the middle of the cheek and extend slightly upward to the end of the wing where the tips meet, a little above the wing. In many patterns the horns are simply left out due to the scarcity of materials.

3

Simple Strip-Wing Flies

Many of the popular flies used in salmon fishing today are dressings consisting of a plain body with a throat hackle in front and a simple feather strip wing that seem very closely related to the ordinary trout wet fly. In earlier years of salmon fishing these "small summer patterns," as the British call them, were designed for fishing during the summer months, when most salmon are deep in holding pools and smaller flies are needed. The sparseness of these simple feather wings dressed on small hooks allowed them to sink much deeper and faster than the fully dressed flies, without alarming the fish.

The modern angler, however, does not reserve his use of strip-wing flies just for such conditions, but has found them effective almost any time if a few alterations are made in their style. The fly dresser can regulate the sink rate and visibility by applying heavier dressing on larger single or double hooks, thereby making them suitable for fishing at any level, regardless of river conditions.

There are many such strip-wing patterns. Some have gained popularity at a local level and remained there, while others were picked up by visiting anglers and passed along as they gained recognition and sometimes fame.

Because of the distinct difference, not only in material, but also in material application, I have picked two patterns among the many used today for this important first practice in salmon fly dressing: the Blue Charm, a British pattern that long ago earned its "classic" status and well-deserved place among the best of salmon flies; and the Crossfield, an Icelandic fly of considerable fame.

Before getting down to the business of dressing these two flies—or any other salmon fly—it is important that you study the previous chapters dealing with materials, anatomy, and proportions. Some of these simple feather wings may

51

look a lot like ordinary trout wet flies, but one should not be led to believe that they are tied the same way. That would be too simple and, of course, somewhat belittling in view of the tradition attached to such fine flies. Each of the step-by-step instructions that follow use the anatomical terms that are standard on most of the flies you will deal with throughout this book. They must therefore be practiced and learned well if you expect the result of your efforts to resemble a "well-dressed" salmon fly.

TYING IN BODY MATERIALS

Because of the amount of material in salmon flies it becomes most important that the body materials are fastened on the shank at a specific spot. This can often cause difficulties if one does not have steady hands. The following technique can be used for such materials as tinsel, floss, wool, and chenille.

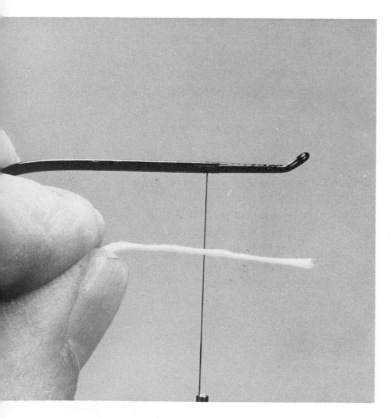

1. Wind the tying thread to the exact position where the material is to be fastened. Cut a length of the material you are going to tie in and hold it horizontally against the near side of the tying thread, with one and a half inches exposed in front of your fingers.

2. Now double the material back to the left, behind the tying thread, and grasp the end with your fingertips, thus forming a loop around the tying thread with the material.

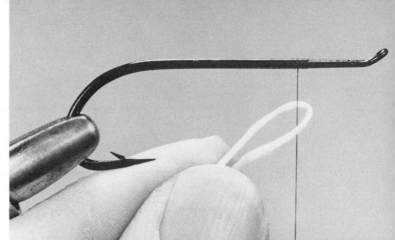

3. Hold the tying thread toward you while sliding the "looped" material up the thread until it reaches the hook shank.

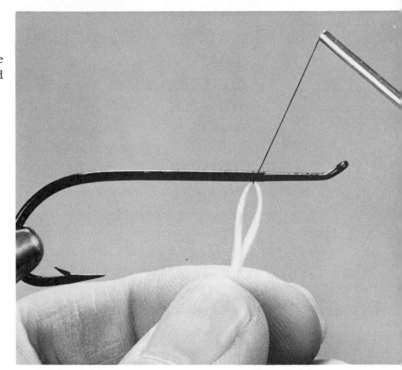

4. Start winding the thread, and when the first turn is almost completed, release the material end and pull gently toward the rear with the long end to open up the loop. Take a few extra turns of thread, and the material is fastened. If the material is to be fastened directly under the shank, hold the loop vertically under the shank as you start to wind the thread; if it is to sit on the far side, hold the loop farther toward the far side.

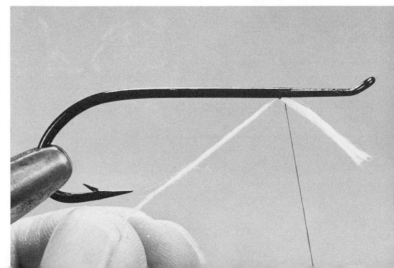

Dressing the Blue Charm

(Feather Wing)

THREAD:	Black, prewaxed 6/0
TAG:	Fine oval silver and golden yellow floss
TAIL:	Golden pheasant crest
BUTT:	Black ostrich herl (sometimes omitted)
BODY:	Black floss
RIBBING:	Oval silver tinsel
THROAT:	A deep-blue-dyed hackle
WING:	Brown-mottled turkey tail, with narrow strips of teal on each side set on the upper half of the wing
TOPPING:	A golden pheasant crest feather
HEAD:	Black thread

I prefer an underwing of eastern pine squirrel tail before I dress the main wing. This makes the wing more durable and easier to set.

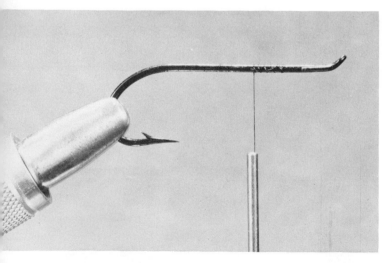

TYING IN THE TAG— Single and Double Hook

1. Place a size 2 single hook firmly in the vise with the shank at a horizontal level and the barb clearly exposed, as shown in the photograph. The exposed barb acts as guidepost for positioning the tag, which in turn determines the style and overall proportions for most salmon flies. Now attach your tying thread in the middle of the hook shank in the usual manner and let it hang by the weight of the bobbin.

2. Take a four-inch length of fine oval silver tinsel for the tag and tie it in under the hook shank with the longest end projecting toward the rear. Do not cut the surplus end.

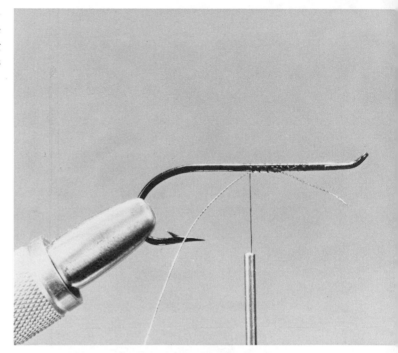

3. Wind the tying thread toward the rear, binding down the tinsel on the underside of the hook shank in the process. Stop at a position directly above the point of the barb, and take two or three extra tight turns before winding it very slightly back towards the eye. Now take one full turn of the tinsel, followed by two more turns wound tight and close up to the right of the first one. Tie off the tinsel on the underside of the shank with two or three turns of thread up against the tag; then wind it forward to a position above the point of the hook, again binding the tinsel end under the shank for the short distance. Do not cut the surplus tinsel.

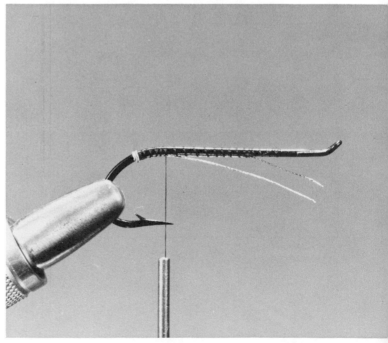

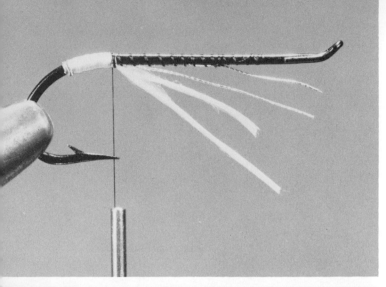

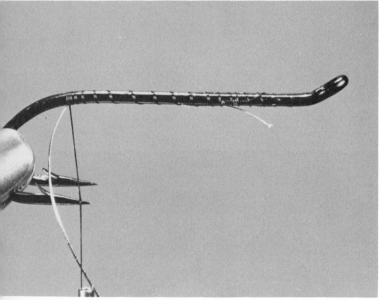

4. Tie in a three-inch length of golden yellow floss on the underside of the shank directly above the hook point. The shortest end must project forward to the hook eye. Grasp the long end and wind it flat and smooth back to and tight against the silver tag and then back over the first layer to the tie-in point. Tie it off under the shank with two or three tight turns of thread. Do not cut the surplus floss end. This finishes the tag, and the tying thread should hang by the bobbin directly in front of the floss segment where the tail is tied in next.

TYING THE DOUBLE-HOOK TAG

5. When dressing the fly on a double hook, I secure it in the vise by the bend nearest to me and adjust the vise head to level the hook. The barb should be visible. The oval tinsel is attached in the same manner as on a single hook. Hold the tinsel toward the rear along the underside of the shank and wind the thread over it in the same direction, to a position directly above a point midway between the hook point and the point of the barb. Take a couple of extra tight turns at that spot.

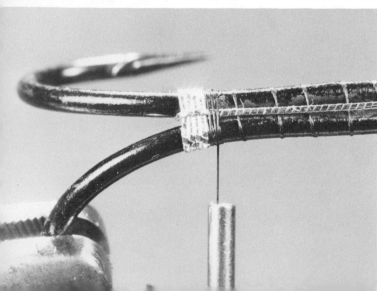

6. Grasp the tinsel and take three or four turns tight against each other working to the left. After the last turn, take the tinsel up between the two hook bends and pull it tight. To secure the end, hold it over the tag to the right and tie it off on top of the shank, directly in front of the first winding. The floss segment can now be applied in the same manner as explained for the single hook.

PREPARING AND TYING IN THE TAIL

7. Select the tail feather from a whole head of crest of a golden pheasant. For a size 2 hook, I pick one that is about 1 to 1¼ inches long. The feather should be full, firm, and fairly straight, with a natural curve. Make sure the fibers at the tip are even and have not been damaged.

8. Prepare the crest feather by pulling off the soft fluff and stray fibers at the base, then moisten your fingers and stroke the feather until the fibers stick together side by side so it appears rather flat. Make sure it is not too sparse for the size fly being dressed.

9. Set the crest feather on top of the hook and gauge the length, which will vary depending on the size fly and the style in which it is being dressed. For a size 2 regular-length hook with the body tied full, which means that the tag is applied to occupy the space from above the point of the barb to above the hook point, the tail should reach just slightly beyond the hook bend, or approximately one-and-a-half hook gaps measured from the tie-in spot, which is directly in front of the floss segment. Hold the tail and take two complete turns of tying thread without pulling them tight. When the second turn is taken, come all the way around so the thread and bobbin are above the hook shank. Now tighten the windings with an upward pull before adding three or four extra turns, tightening those in the same manner. This eliminates the risk of pulling the feather out of line when the thread is tightened, which often happens on a downward pull. Do not trim the surplus feather.

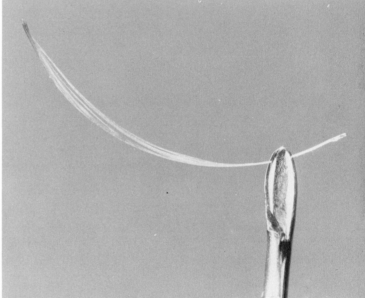

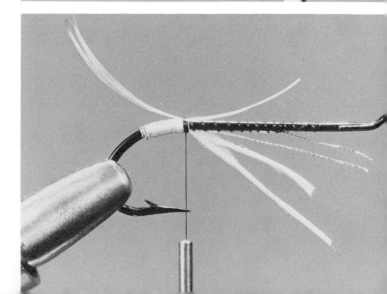

P. 57

TYING IN THE HERL BUTT

10. Select a medium-sized black ostrich herl and study it under a magnifying glass. You will note that the structure is such that all the flues are standing on edge of the stem. Hold the herl on the side of the hook with the flues against the shank and the bare side of the stem out. Fasten it in the same spot as the tail with a couple of turns of thread. When the first winding is applied, the stem will "roll" toward the top of the shank. The herl is thus turned so the stem side, without the flues, is toward the front, and the flues on the rear edge are perpendicular to the shank.

11. Wind the tying thread just very slightly to the right of where the herl is tied in; then grasp the herl with your fingers and wind four to five close turns on the hook to the right without overlapping, much like you would an ordinary hackle. Tie it off with a couple of turns of thread, and the butt is finished. Do not cut the surplus.

TYING IN THE BODY AND RIBBING

12. Tie in a four-inch length of medium oval silver tinsel for the ribbing. Position it on the underside of the shank directly in front of the herl butt. When you have fastened it with a couple of turns of tying thread, take the long end under the hook to the far side and hold it up on an angle while taking a couple of tight turns of thread at the tie-in spot. The tinsel is thus fastened more on the far side of the hook shank rather than directly under it. So, when the ribbing is wound and pulled tight, it will slide down to the correct position—directly under the body where the first turn is supposed to start.

13. After tying in the ribbing tinsel, it is time to cut all the surplus ends that are now going to serve as an underbody. Trim all the ends to about one-fourth of a hook length short of the hook eye. Now wind the thread over the ends and bind them down on the shank; make sure they don't twist around. Go back and forth with the tying thread if necessary. This method eliminates the bumps and unevenness that might otherwise occur if the surplus was cut close to where it was tied in. Once you get used to this you can cut each material end to the specified length one at a time as they are tied in. Now tie in an eight-inch length of black floss in front, as in the photograph.

14. Wind the floss smoothly to the rear, up against the butt, then back to the tie-in position and tie it off. Make sure there is plenty of room in front for the other materials and the head, then cut the surplus. Spiral the ribbing forward over the body to the front, taking <u>five turns only</u>. Tie off the ribbing tinsel under the shank and trim the surplus.

TYING IN THE THROAT HACKLE

The throat hackle on a salmon fly is a relatively simple affair consisting of a bunch of hackle fibers tied under the hook shank in front and slanting gently back in the direction of the hook point. A few fibers are allowed to expand halfway up on each side of the body at the tie-in spot. Actually, a throat hackle, when tied in correctly, will encircle the lower half of the hook circumference rather than just sit directly underneath and will be one and one-half times the hook gap in length.

Since the material lists for some patterns featured in this book were written many years ago, you will often read that the hackle should be wound as a collar and then be tied down as a throat. However, I have never understood why it should be necessary to first wind it as a collar when most fibers ultimately end up underneath except, perhaps, in the case of very large flies where lots of throat hackle is needed and the bulk of the hackle stem is of little consequence. Therefore, I do not use the old method of winding the hackle first. Instead, I have perfected a "false hackling" method where bunches of hackle fibers are tied in to form the throat. This not only looks better and is less bulky, but it requires very little time in selecting the right size hackle feather.

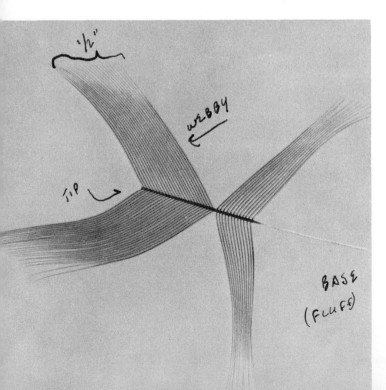

15. To prepare a false hackle for the throat on a Blue Charm I use a soft, blue-dyed body feather or short, firm saddle hackle with the webby fibers at the base as long as the body of the fly being dressed, in this case a size 2. Pull off the fluff and leave the stem bare to where the first usable fibers are located. Now cut away the tip portion of the hackle, leaving only a half-inch section with webby fibers located on both sides of the stem directly across from each other. Separate the fibers as shown in the photograph; stroke one-third of them in the direction of the bare stem and the other two-thirds the opposite way. The feather is now ready to be tied in.

16. Tie in the prepared feather section with three turns of thread, as shown. The windings at this point should not be pulled too tight. The section should sit under the shank with the best side out and the largest bunch of fibers projecting toward the rear. If the throat at this time appears to be a little sparse, take it off and tie in another one, using two hackles prepared at the same time and tied in together.

17. Pull the stem carefully to the right, guiding it with your fingers while drawing the hackle fibers into place directly under the hook shank. The length of the throat should be one and one-half hook gaps, and it should slant back toward the point of the hook. Press a little with your fingernail at the tie-in spot so all the fibers are well spread out and sitting parallel with the body when viewed from below. Now secure the fibers tightly with a couple of extra turns of thread before trimming away the surplus close in front of the windings. Do not discard the surplus; it is used in the next step.

18. The remainder from the previous step is now prepared by trimming away the little triangle in front of the feather section. Tie in one bunch of fibers on the right side (near side) first, as shown in the photograph. Note that the fibers are tied in so they start in the middle of the side and blend into the other throat fibers underneath. Secure the fibers tightly with a couple of thread windings and trim off the surplus close in front of the tie-in spot.

19. Now tie in the rest of the fibers on the left side in a similar manner, then trim the surplus. The "false" throat hackle is completed.

PREPARING AND TYING IN THE WING

Tying the wing on a salmon fly is by no means an easy task, and even the simplest strip wing, such as the one used on the Blue Charm, Crossfield, and many others, can often cause problems initially, even for the experienced fly dresser.

There are, however, some basic steps that tend to make things a little easier. First, one must recognize that there are two sides to a feather wing, usually referred to in fly dressing as the "near" and "far" wing. For the purpose of selecting the proper feather strips, both for the simple flies and the more complex dressings that follow later in the book, we will refer to them as the "right" and "left" wing. The right one is the wing nearest to you if you are a right-handed tier, and the "left" one for obvious reasons is the one on the other side.

The second thing one must recognize is the structural difference in the feathers that are used for winging. Regardless of the species of bird, feathers can generally be divided into two categories: those with the quill stem in the middle where the fibers on either side of the stem are of equal length, color, and texture, and those with a quill stem somewhat offset from the center where only one side is usable. Shown in the photograph are two typical feathers with the quill stem in the center, each of which will make a complete wing. The left one is a six-inch-long, brown-mottled turkey tail feather and the other a teal

20. Feathers with the quill stem in the center.

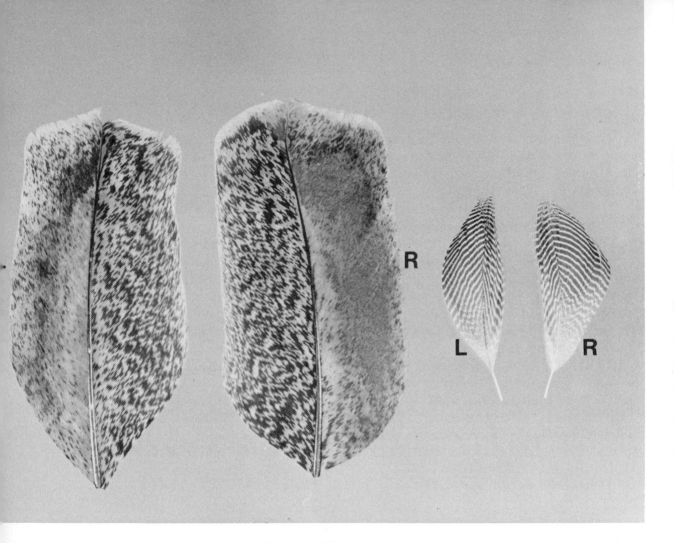

21. Feathers with off-center quill stems.

body feather. The feathers are shown with their best sides up and are marked "left" and "right" merely to illustrate the respective sides of the feather. It does not necessarily mean left and right wing on the fly. The two feathers on the left in the next photograph are brown-mottled turkey secondary flight feathers, one from the left wing and one from the right wing. The flank feathers in the same photograph are taken from the left and right sides of the bird. Unlike those with the stem in the center, you will need a pair of feathers to complete a wing. In addition to the winging method described step by step in this chapter, there is an alternate, but certainly not secondary, method described in chapter 4 under dressing the fully dressed Black Doctor. Either of the two methods can be used for dressing any of the feather-wing flies.

22. Tie in a small bunch of gray squirrel tail as an underwing to support the fragile feathers that will form the main wing. (See chapter 6 for instructions.) The tips of the hair should reach to about the middle of the tail. You will note that the butt ends are not tapered but cut directly across before applying a little cement and tying them in. This makes it easier to form the short, stubby head later on, for which, you will note, I have left room in front.

23. Cut a segment from a small, brown-mottled turkey tail feather, as shown in the photograph. I prefer the feather with the stem in the middle whenever possible. The strips represent the right and left wing and should be exactly the same width, about one-quarter inch for a size 2 hook. The length of the strips should be chosen so they do not exceed one and a half wing lengths at the very most. If they are too long, they greatly affect the curvature, and the feather may collapse when tied in. I prefer not to separate the strips before I tie them in, but it is perfectly all right to do so by splitting the stem and leaving a half stem on each strip to hold them together.

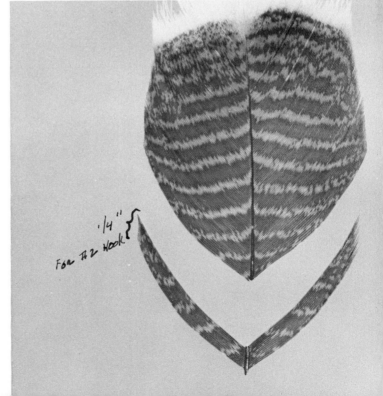

24. The feather strips should now be "humped" to give the wing a low horizontal profile when tied in. Hold the left feather strip between your thumb and index finger as shown, then stroke it down a couple of times until it has gained a gentle downward curve. The left strip in this case is tied in as the right wing (the wing nearest to a right-handed tier).

25. Lay the strip along the side of the hook against the underwing, with the tip reaching to just inside the tail; the front of the feather should be slightly down on the side of the hook at the tie-in spot. Hold it in that position until you grasp it with your other hand, as seen in step 26.

26. Place your index finger on the far side of the hook and hold the feather strip against the hook with your thumb on the near side. The fingers should be positioned so the first turn of thread will fall directly in front of and close to the fingertips.

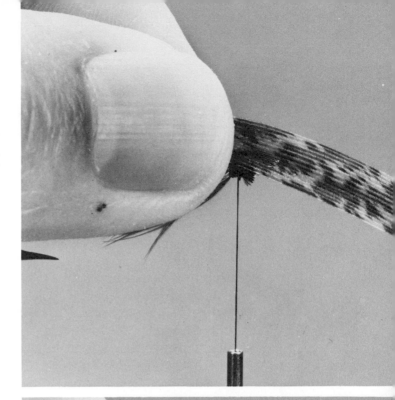

27. Hold the feather strip tightly with your fingers in the exact position shown in step 26. Then take the first turn of tying thread slowly over the wing strip, while your index finger prevents it from being pulled over the top of the hook. Allow the thread to roll the upper edge of the wing slightly, so that it falls in the middle, longitudinally, of the hook shank. Now take a second complete turn of thread and come all the way around so both thread and bobbin are above the wing. At this point, tighten the thread windings with a slow upward pull while holding the wing strip firmly in place; then add three or four more turns to secure it tightly. Hold the wing while trimming the surplus end directly across close to the windings. The wing should now sit as shown in step 32. It is important to note that the wing is sitting slightly down on the side and not directly on top of the hook, and that the space in front allotted for the head is not lost.

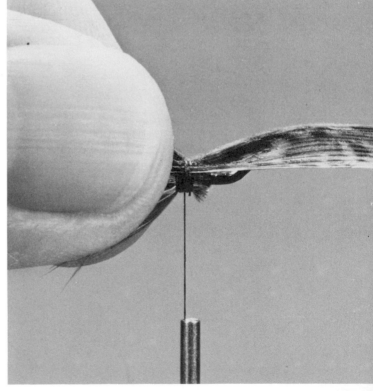

REVERSING THE TYING THREAD

Before we procede to tie in the left wing strip, the tying thread must be reversed to a counterclockwise direction so that the left wing can be rolled into place by the thread, which is coming from *under* the hook, just as it was for the right wing. This gives the wing a good symmetrical balance and prevents the left wing from accidentally being doubled up or bent by the thread as it passes over top of the hook.

Reversing the thread will usually apply only to setting the main wing when it consists of feather, single strips, or married fibers. After the left wing is tied in, the thread is reversed back to its normal clockwise direction. For the purposes of illustration, this technique will be shown on a "practice" hook dressed with a dark underwing using white thread.

28. Cross the tying thread forward on the near side and take one complete turn of thread directly in front of the wing stumps.

29. Release six to eight inches of tying thread and double it over your finger, back to its base, and *under* the hook shank. At this point take two turns of thread counterclockwise on the hook shank while still holding the thread loop with your fingers.

30. Take your finger out of the loop and twist it together. Hold the twisted thread above the hook at an angle toward the rear on the near side.

31. Wind the tying thread counterclockwise back to the first windings that secured the right wing; bind down the twisted thread loop in the process. The loop can now be trimmed away with your scissors, and the reversing procedure is completed.

REVERSING IT BACK

To reverse the thread back to a clockwise direction, use the same steps as before, but with the following changes: (1) cross the thread on the far side; (2) take the thread back to the base and *over* the hook shank.

32. When the tying thread has been reversed to a counterclockwise direction, hump the left wing strip and tie it in on the far side by holding it in the same manner as when tying in the right one. In this case the thumb pressure will prevent the feather from rolling over the shank. Now hold the wing in position while trimming away the surplus end close to the thread windings. Before going to the next step, reverse the tying thread back to its original clockwise direction.

(33.) If tied in correctly, the upper edges of the wing strips will meet lengthwise directly over the center of the hook shank, as shown in this top view.

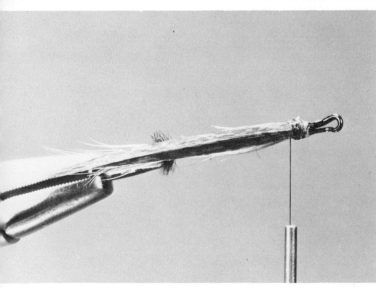

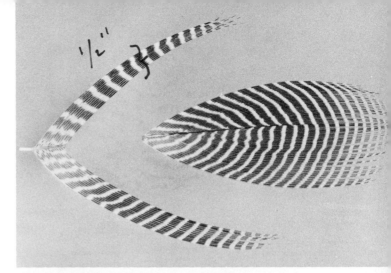

34. The teal strips are now prepared from a feather with the quill stem in the center, as shown in the photograph. The strips should be chosen so they will reach to the tip of the turkey wing that is already tied in. The width of the strips for a size 2 hook should be one-eighth inch before humping.

35. Tie in the teal strips on the right and left sides by using the instructions in steps 24, 25, 26, and 27. Since the strips will cover the upper half of the turkey wing, it is not necessary to hold them down on the sides as much as indicated for the turkey strips. Nor is it necessary to reverse the tying thread. Trim the surplus ends, and you are ready to tie in the topping.

PREPARING AND TYING IN THE TOPPING

The golden pheasant crest feather tied in over the wing as a "topping" is often the hallmark by which a salmon fly can be recognized. It serves the purpose of holding the wing together and gives a bright, translucent effect to the upper perimeter of the wing. The latter, in my opinion, is the only task it truly performs satisfactorily. The topping extends from the tie-in position at the head to where it meets with the tip of the tail in the rear. For this reason the crest feather must be carefully chosen, preferably from a whole "head of crests," as when choosing the tail feather. (See step 1 for tying in the tail).

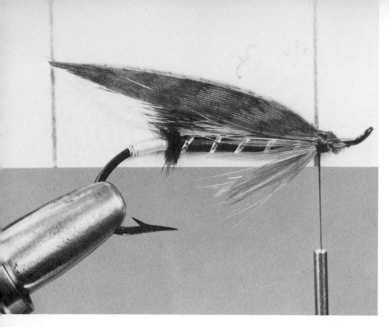

36. To determine the length of the topping for a particular size fly I have found it most practical to hold a small piece of cardboard behind the fly and make a couple of pencil marks: one at the tie-in spot in front, and a second where the topping meets the tip of the tail. If you practice enough you will soon discover that you can pick the right size crest feather without using such a device.

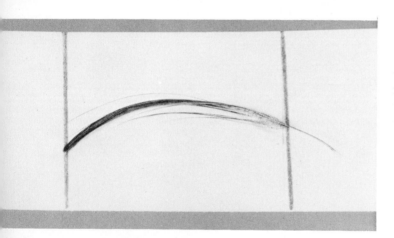

37. Choose a crest that is just slightly longer than the measurement on the cardboard, and pull the fuzz and short, unwanted fibers from the butt end. The remaining fibers, still with a small portion of the web, should now be the exact length of the topping.

38. The crest you have picked and prepared will rarely have the right curvature in relation to the upper perimeter of the wing. To correct this I soak the crest in water for a few minutes, then place it to dry on an object with a curvature similar to that of the wing. A water glass, round jar, or bottle will do nicely. Make sure the crest is lying straight lengthwise with all the fibers closely bunched next to one another. When the crest is dry, it should have the same curvature as the object on which it was dried.

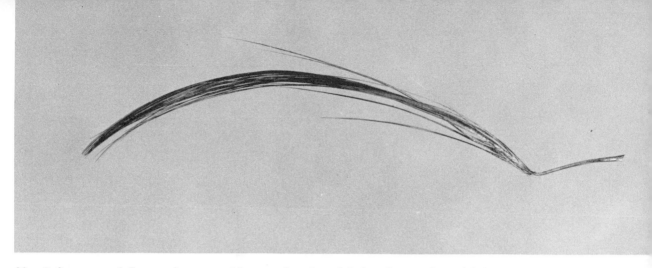

39. Soften up and flatten the stem with your thumb and index finger, then nick it with your thumbnail close to the lowest fibers and bend the stem to an angle, as shown in the photograph. This is done so the crest will sit with a nice slope over the wing when tied in.

40. Tie in the topping with a few turns of thread and align it so it runs lengthwise on top of the wing and meets the tip of the tail. When well aligned, fasten it securely with several tight turns of thread. Hold the feather in place with your fingers and trim the surplus end. This finishes the fly as such, and we are ready to wind the head.

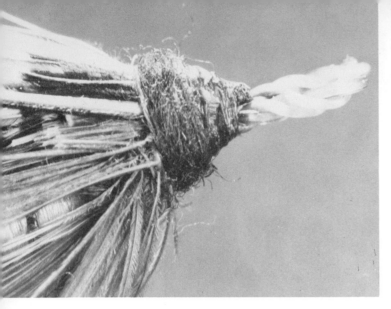

The short, stubby head of an old fly has the same basic shape as a modern lacquered one.

FINISHING THE HEAD

The head is just as important as any other part of a well-dressed salmon fly. If you study the photograph of the old fly you will see the unique shape, which can be best described as short and stubby and, in those days, unlacquered. The shape has not changed much over the years, but the use of thinner thread gives the tier an opportunity to form a very smooth head that can be lacquered to a nice shine.

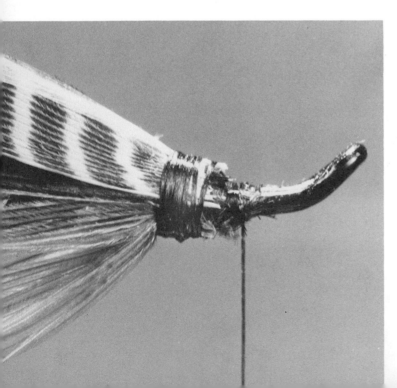

41. After trimming all the ends, it is best to spiral the thread over the butt ends to directly in front of them. Apply pressure on the tying thread and start winding toward the rear, binding down the butt ends tight, and thus starting the taper from the front.

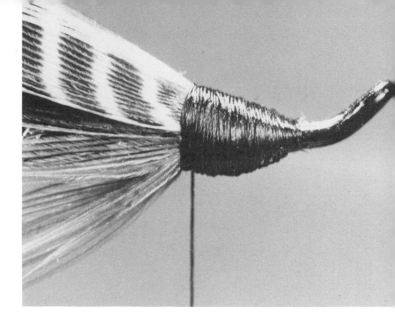

42. Continue to apply tying thread to form the head, as shown in the photograph. The last turn is applied tightly to the rear of the head while holding the wing structure sandwiched between your thumb and first finger with a slight upward pressure.

43. Take five or six whip-finishing turns and pull them tight. Now apply a lot of tension on the thread and cut it close to the head. The tension applied will make the thread end retract and blend with the rest of the windings. Some tiers will often break the thread deliberately when pulling the whip finish tight and achieve the same result. This method, however, requires a bit of practice. After cutting the thread you should apply several coats of fine, clear lacquer, which finishes the fly.

Dressing the Teal=Winged Crossfield

THREAD:	Black, prewaxed 6/0
TAG:	Fine oval silver tinsel
TAIL:	Golden pheasant crest
BODY:	Embossed silver tinsel
THROAT:	Medium-blue-dyed hackle
WING:	Black-barred teal over an underwing of brown-mottled turkey tail
HEAD:	Black

For this fly I use a small bunch of white-tipped squirrel tail under the brown-mottled turkey tail for winging.

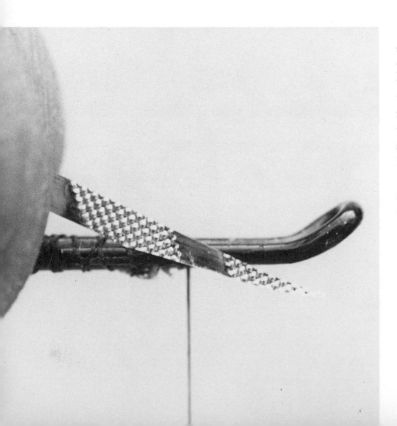

1. The procedure for tying the body of this fly is essentially the same as already explained in dressing the Blue Charm, with the notable difference that it is made of tinsel, floss is absent in the tag, and there is no herl butt. As a result, a few more silver windings have been applied, and the tag should occupy only a space from above the hook point to midway between the hook point and the point of the barb, as seen in step 2. With such an arrangement the tail on the fly should reach only to the bend. Like the floss on the Blue Charm, the embossed tinsel is tied on in front. Before tying in the tinsel, taper it as shown in the photo.

2. Fasten it in the middle of the taper, so it will be easier to start when winding it, particularly if the silver is very wide. When it is tied in, cover the point of the taper so it won't accidentally cut the thread. It is wound to the rear and then forward over the first layer and tied off at the tie-in spot before the throat is applied. Care should be taken that silver windings are laid side by side and do not overlap. The two layers should prevent any noticeable gaps.

3. Tie in a small bunch of white-tipped squirrel tail with a turkey strip on each side, using the same instructions as in the Blue Charm.

TYING IN THE TEAL WING

This type of wing is the one I am most often asked to do when demonstrating salmon fly tying, and for good reason. It is a very difficult technique mainly because the teal feather itself is fragile, often collapses completely when tied in, and ends up with the well-known "paint brush" look. The best way I have found to eliminate this unfortunate situation is to make a suitable underwing such as the one described in step 3, and then prepare the teal feather in the following manner:

4. Select a firm teal feather where the fibers on each side of the center quill are the same length. Make sure the feather is large enough to comply with the measurements that follow, which are gauged to a size 2 hook.

Measure a wing length from the tip of the feather down the middle and cut the stem, thus forming an open V shape. Now measure one-half-inch down the stem from the bottom of the V and tear off all the fibers that are below. The feather is now ready to be tied in. I should like to mention that the one-half-inch measurement gradually gets smaller when you dress smaller flies. Some experimentation in those cases is needed to determine the correct measurement.

5. Moisten your fingers a little and stroke down the feather so that all the fibers are lying next to one another, and at the same time see that the V is closed considerably. This makes the feather easier to manipulate when folded over the underwing and tied down.

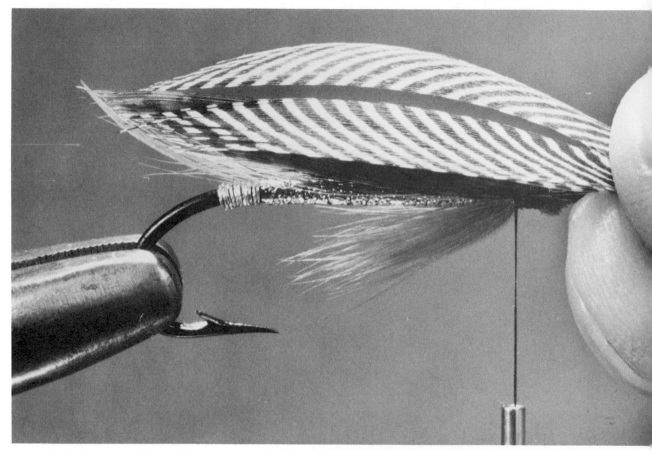

6. Hold the feather flat over the body, as shown, with the tips reaching to just inside the tail. Carefully fold the teal strips down on each side of the underwing. This is done simultaneously—the near side with your thumb, the far side with your index finger. Hold them tight in that position with your fingers right at the tie-in spot.

7. Take the first turn of thread slowly over the feather and bind it down on the shank, followed by three or four more tight turns while still holding the wings.

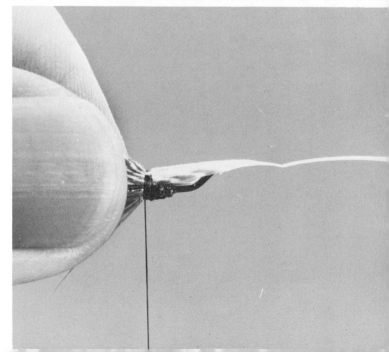

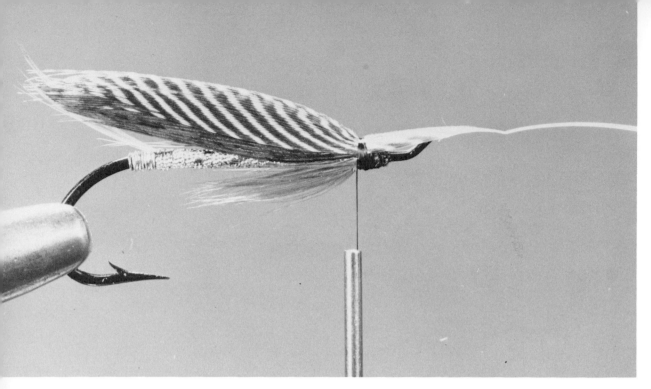

8. Inspect the wings on both sides and pull possible stray fibers into place.

9. Trim away the surplus and wind the head. Now lacquer the head, and the fly is finished.

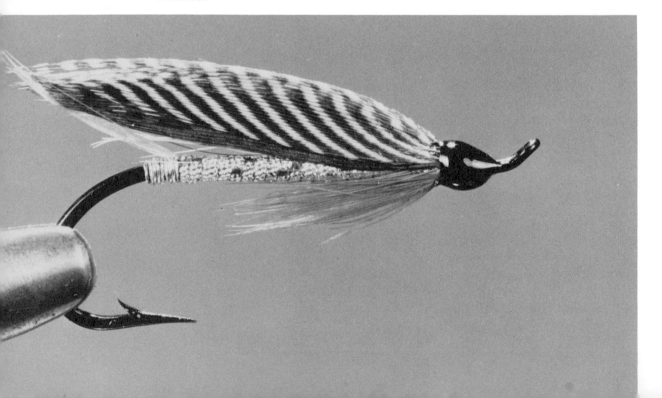

SELECTED SIMPLE STRIP-WING PATTERNS

Important note: Some of the feathers mentioned in the dressings are no longer available, and a substitute may be needed as suggested in chapter 1. Since the tying instructions in the preceding text were limited to the very basic parts of a salmon fly, it may be necessary to study the chapter on fully dressed flies in order to dress several of the flies included in the following list of patterns.

Amethyst

THREAD:	Black, prewaxed 6/0
TAIL:	Golden pheasant crest
BODY:	In four equal sections of orange, magenta, green, and blue floss
RIBBING:	Oval gold tinsel
THROAT:	Soft black hackle
WING:	Dark-brown mottled turkey tail
HEAD:	Black tying thread

Art Lee

THREAD:	Black, prewaxed 6/0
TAG:	Fine oval silver tinsel
TAIL:	Golden pheasant crest
BUTT:	Black wool or ostrich herl
BODY:	Golden yellow floss
RIBBING:	Oval silver tinsel
THROAT:	Black hackle

WING:	Two sections of claret-dyed goose with broad strips of teal flank feather on each side, as long as underwing
SIDES:	Jungle cock
HEAD:	Black ostrich herl on half close to wing; front half is black tying thread

This fly was originated by Icelandic Gillie Thordur Pethrsson on the upper Laxa I Adaldal in honor of my good friend Art Lee. Thordur used Art's clothing as a color scheme for the dressing.

Badger

THREAD:	Black, prewaxed 6/0
TAG:	Fine oval or round silver tinsel
TAIL:	Golden pheasant crest and tippet in strands
BODY:	Crimson seal's fur or Seal-Ex dubbing
RIBBING:	Oval silver tinsel
THROAT:	Badger hackle
WING:	Two sections of light mottled turkey tail
HEAD:	Black tying thread

Black Fairy

THREAD:	Black, prewaxed 6/0
TAG:	Fine oval silver tinsel and yellow floss
TAIL:	Golden pheasant crest
BUTT:	Black ostrich herl
BODY:	Black seal's fur or Seal-Ex dubbing
RIBBING:	Oval gold tinsel
THROAT:	Black hackle
WING:	Brown mallard, two sections set low
HEAD:	Black tying thread

Bastard Dose

THREAD:	Black, prewaxed 6/0
TAG:	Fine oval silver tinsel and golden yellow floss
TAIL:	Golden pheasant crest
BUTT:	Black ostrich herl
BODY:	Rear quarter, light blue seal's fur or Seal-Ex; remainder, black seal's fur or Seal-Ex dubbing
RIBBING:	Oval silver tinsel
THROAT:	Claret-dyed hackle
WING:	Two tippets back to back veiled with wide double strips of teal on each side
TOPPING:	Golden pheasant crest
HEAD:	Black tying thread

Black Spean

THREAD:	Black, prewaxed 6/0
TAG:	Fine oval silver tinsel and lemon floss
TAIL:	Golden pheasant crest
BODY:	Black seal's fur or Seal-Ex dubbing
RIBBING:	Oval gold tinsel
THROAT:	Speckled guinea fowl
WING:	Two sections of brown mallard set low
HEAD:	Black tying thread

Blue Charm

See tying instructions and material list in this chapter.

Chalmers

THREAD:	Black, prewaxed 6/0
TAG:	Fine oval silver tinsel and yellow floss
TAIL:	Golden pheasant crest
BUTT:	Black ostrich herl
BODY:	Magenta floss
RIBBING:	Oval silver tinsel
THROAT:	Magenta-dyed hackle
WING:	Two sections of brown mottled turkey tail
SIDES:	Jungle cock
TOPPING:	Golden pheasant crest
HEAD:	Black tying thread

Cinnamon Turkey

THREAD:	Black, prewaxed 6/0
TAG:	Fine round silver tinsel and yellow floss
TAIL:	Golden pheasant crest and scarlet ibis
BODY:	Rear quarter, half yellow and half red seal's fur or Seal-Ex dubbing; remainder, black seal's fur or Seal-Ex
RIBBING:	Flat silver tinsel
THROAT:	Dark blue-dyed hackle
WING:	Teal over tippet in strands, veiled both sides with cinnamon turkey tail
TOPPING:	Golden pheasant crest
HEAD:	Black tying thread

Claret Alder

See pattern in chapter 5.

Crossfield

See material list for dressing the Teal-Winged Crossfield in this chapter.

Dreadnought

THREAD:	Black, prewaxed 6/0
TAG:	Flat gold tinsel
TAIL:	Golden pheasant crest and Indian crow
BUTT:	Scarlet wool or Seal-Ex dubbing
BODY:	Three equal sections of oval silver tinsel; rear section butted with fiery brown; middle section butted with dark blue seal's fur or Seal-Ex dubbing
THROAT:	Magenta- and deep blue-dyed hackle, mixed
WING:	Two sections of cinnamon turkey tail
SIDES:	Jungle cock
HORNS:	Red macaw
HEAD:	Black tying thread

This fly is also attractive if dressed with a wing of light-brown mottled turkey tail with white tip.

Jeannie

See pattern in chapter 5.

Elver

THREAD:	Black, prewaxed 6/0
BODY:	Black floss
RIBBING:	Oval silver tinsel
WING:	Two blue, white-striped vulturine guinea fowl feathers, twice as long as the hook and set on edge along each side of body
HACKLE:	Plain blue vulturine body feather wound as a collar and tied back to blend with the wing
HEAD:	Red tying thread

Furnace Brown

THREAD:	Black, prewaxed 6/0
TAG:	Fine oval silver tinsel and golden yellow floss
TAIL:	Golden pheasant and tippet in strands
BODY:	Rear one quarter, bright orange seal's fur; remainder, fiery brown seal's fur or Seal-Ex dubbing; heavily picked out underneath
RIBBING:	Oval gold tinsel
HACKLE:	Furnace hackle
THROAT:	Extra turns of furnace hackle wound in front and tied under as a throat
WING:	Two brown mallard strips set low
HEAD:	Black tying thread

Green Peacock

See pattern in chapter 5.

Goldfinch

THREAD:	Black, prewaxed 6/0
TAG:	Fine oval silver tinsel and yellow floss
TAIL:	Golden pheasant crest
BUTT:	Black ostrich herl
BODY:	Flat gold tinsel
RIBBING:	Oval gold tinsel
HACKLE:	Claret-dyed hackle
THROAT:	Guinea fowl, dyed blue (substitute for jay)
WING:	Tippet in strands, over which are married strips of yellow and red swan or goose; yellow strip twice as wide as the red
CHEEKS:	Indian crow
TOPPING:	Golden pheasant crest (sometimes two or three)
HEAD:	Black tying thread

Helmsdale

THREAD:	Black, prewaxed 6/0
TAG:	Fine oval silver tinsel and orange floss
TAIL:	Golden pheasant crest
BUTT:	Black ostrich herl
BODY:	Rear fifth, yellow floss; remainder, yellow seal's fur or Seal-Ex dubbing
RIBBING:	Oval silver tinsel
HACKLE:	Yellow hackle
THROAT:	Light-blue-dyed hackle
WING:	Two sections of brown mottled turkey tail
HEAD:	Black tying thread

Jockie

THREAD:	Black, prewaxed 6/0
TAG:	Fine round or oval silver tinsel
TAIL:	Golden pheasant crest and Indian crow
BODY:	Rear third, yellow floss; remainder, dark claret floss
RIBBING:	Oval silver tinsel
THROAT:	Coch-y-bondhu hackle
WING:	Two strips of brown mallard
SIDES:	Jungle cock
HEAD:	Black tying thread

March Brown

See pattern in chapter 5.

Mignon

THREAD:	Black, prewaxed 6/0
TAG:	Fine oval silver tinsel and yellow floss
TAIL:	Golden pheasant crest and strands of teal flank
BUTT:	Black ostrich herl
BODY:	Claret chenille
HACKLE:	Claret-dyed hackle
THROAT:	Gray heron and teal
WING:	Two sections of gray wing or tail feather
HEAD:	Black tying thread

Mitchell

THREAD:	Black, prewaxed 6/0
TAG:	Fine oval silver tinsel and golden yellow floss
TAIL:	Golden pheasant crest and blue kingfisher
BUTT:	Black ostrich herl
BODY:	Rear fifth, golden yellow floss butted with red-dyed ostrich herl; remainder, black floss
RIBBING:	Oval silver tinsel over black floss
THROAT:	Yellow-dyed hackle fronted with black hackle
WING:	Two sections of black crow wing feather
SIDES:	Jungle cock
CHEEKS:	Blue kingfisher
TOPPING:	Golden pheasant crest
HEAD:	Black with a red band close to wing (The red band can be applied with red tying thread.)

Night Hawk

THREAD:	Black, prewaxed 6/0
TAG:	Fine oval silver tinsel and yellow floss
TAIL:	Golden pheasant crest and blue kingfisher
BUTT:	Red wool or Seal-Ex dubbing
BODY:	Flat silver tinsel
RIBBING:	Oval silver tinsel
THROAT:	Black hackle
WING:	Two sections of black turkey or crow
SIDES:	Jungle cock
CHEEKS:	Blue kingfisher
TOPPING:	Golden pheasant crest
HEAD:	Red tying thread

Oriole

THREAD:	Black, prewaxed 6/0
TAIL:	Small bunch of fibers from golden pheasant breast feather
BODY:	Black Seal-Ex dubbing, dressed smooth
RIBBING:	Oval silver tinsel, first two turns wound at the tail as a tag
THROAT:	Brown hackle
WING:	A good bunch of fibers from a golden pheasant breast feather, on each side of which are double strips of gray mallard flank feather dyed pale olive green
HEAD:	Black tying thread

Sheriff

THREAD:	Black, prewaxed 6/0
TAG:	Fine oval gold tinsel
TAIL:	Golden pheasant crest and small bunch of fibers from speckled guinea fowl
BUTT:	Black ostrich herl
BODY:	Rear half, flat gold tinsel; front half, black ostrich herl
RIBBING:	Oval gold tinsel
HACKLE:	Yellow-dyed hackle over front body half
THROAT:	Speckled guinea fowl
WING:	Two sections of dark-brown mottled turkey tail, on each side of which are broad strips of brown mallard
SIDES:	Jungle cock, half as long as wing
TOPPING:	Golden pheasant crest
HORNS:	Blue and yellow macaw
HEAD:	Black tying thread

Sweep

THREAD:	Black, prewaxed 6/0
TAG:	Fine oval silver or gold tinsel
TAIL:	Golden pheasant crest
BUTT:	Black ostrich herl
BODY:	Black floss
RIBBING:	Oval silver or gold tinsel
THROAT:	Soft black hackle reaching to hook point
WING:	Two sections of black crow
CHEEKS:	Blue kingfisher
HORNS:	Blue and yellow macaw (often omitted)
HEAD:	Black tying thread

Thunder and Lightning

See pattern in chapter 5.

4

Fully Dressed
Feather Wings

The most remarkable, and the most beautiful, artificial fishing flies an angler can tie to his leader are the fully dressed classics, created for salmon fishing centuries ago. Since the days of Kelson and Pryce-Tannatt over a hundred years ago, when salmon were plentiful and flies meticulously dressed with feathers, silks, and silver from distant corners of the world through the leaner contemporary years of dressings, the fully-dressed flies have never ceased to excite the angler. That applies equally to the fly dresser whose task it is to arrange the ingredients in an orderly fashion on the iron. Their character and style have surely made them as much a part of salmon fishing tradition as fishing itself.

Salmon flies with complicated bodies and wings, such as those in this chapter, have always been considered out of reach for the average flytier, reserved for people with special artistic talent and blessed with extraordinary manual dexterity. This, of course, is a total misconception. Anyone who can tie a decent trout fly can learn to dress a salmon fly. The final outcome of your efforts, however, depends entirely on your willingness to carefully study the proportions and materials and, of course, the degree of fanaticism with which you follow the tying instructions.

Many of the feather wing flies that are referred to as classics or fully-dressed flies are so different in basic design that it was necessary to divide them into groups in order to fully explain the difference in their character, style, and method of dressing. The chapter at hand, for example, deals with those flies that are most often thought of as being the "standard patterns." In other chapters that follow throughout the book you will find the instructions for tying the grubs, prawns, tube flies, Spey flies, — all of which are of great importance in salmon fishing, but which, in the true sense of the meaning, are not really fully dressed.

The fully-dressed flies illustrate more than any other salmon fly grouping the possibilities for experiment that exists in dressing salmon flies. Perhaps one should say exist*ed,* since in the Victorian era of Pryce-Tannatt, when many of these patterns were originated, sometimes seemingly as a rationale for using the latest exotic feathers from the colonies, they had the peculiar habit of becoming instant classics, as if set in fast-drying cement. This kind of elaboration for its own sake is very much out of favor today, but it has left us with an incredible legacy of fully-dressed feather wing patterns of which I have listed only my personal selections. There are hundreds more for the ambitious tier.

THE WHOLE FEATHER WING

This wing style invariably consists of whole feathers as the main ingredients — golden pheasant or Amherst tippets, sword feathers, jungle cock feathers and, on rare occasions, whole hackles — on the outside of which are usually to be found hackles, feather strips, either married strands or whole segments.

Several of the anatomical parts that are more or less standard on salmon flies were discussed in Chapter 3, which in many respects is the most important chapter in the entire book and surely a stepping stone for the chapter at hand. Therefore, this chapter deals in detail only with those applications not previously explained.

Since the day I was asked to dress and photograph an Orange Parson for the cover of *Fly Fisherman Magazine* (Pre-Season Issue, 1977), I have had many requests, not only for flies, but also for the materials list and dressing instructions. It is an appealing fly, to angler and fish alike. I have therefore chosen the Orange Parson as the main exercise for learning to tie the whole feather wing.

Dressing the Orange Parson

(Whole Feather Wing)

THREAD: Black, prewaxed 6/0

TAG: Fine oval silver tinsel (or wire) and lilac floss

TAIL: Golden pheasant crest and tippet in strands

BODY: Orange floss, followed by orange, scarlet, and fiery brown seal's fur in equal sections (Seal-Ex may be used as a substitute)

RIBBING: Oval silver tinsel

BODY HACKLE: A lemon-dyed hackle

THROAT: Cock-of-the-rock   (orange)

WING: Two golden pheasant tippets back to back, veiled each side with cock-of-the-rock

SIDES: Strips of barred woodduck

CHEEKS: Blue chatterer (substitute with kingfisher or blue dyed hen feather)

TOPPING: Two or three golden pheasant crest feathers

HORNS: Blue and yellow macaw (may be omitted)

HEAD: Black tying thread

The orange feathers from cock-of-the-rock are no longer available, and an orange-dyed substitute is used. See dyeing instructions in Chapter 1.

This fly has turned out to be not only a good fish-getter, but the striking color combination lends itself well to display and framing. Since no jungle cock eye is required—a rarity among the classic fully dressed patterns—it can be authentically tied from available materials.

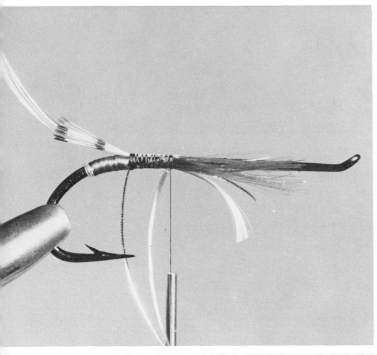

TYING THE BODY

1. For practical reasons, it is best to dress the first fly on a rather large hook, size 2/0 to 3/0, single. This will enable you to better control the various materials, proportions, etc. Tie in the tag so that it starts over the barb of the hook, together with the tail, which in the case of a fly being dressed full should project about half a hook gap beyond the bend. The tippet strands are placed on top of the crest so that they reach to the middle, which is customary when a second material is used in the tail. (See chapter 2.) Now fasten the ribbing under the shank at the same spot and wind the tying thread one-fourth of a hook length forward, where a four-inch length of orange floss is tied in under the shank. (When dividing a body length into segments, the space for the head is excluded.)

2. Wind the orange floss segment so that it occupies a fourth of the body length, then select a lemon-dyed neck hackle and prepare it in the same manner as for the hackle collar explained in chapter 6. The fibers closest to the tip should be slightly shorter than a hook gap. Tie in the hackle directly in front of the orange body segment with the best side up. To facilitate the doubling and winding later, a small portion of stem is left free between the first fibers and the tie-in windings.

3. Wind the tying thread over all the material ends and bind them down on the shank as an underbody. Then take the thread back to directly in front of the orange floss segment. Roll some orange seal fur or Seal-Ex on the tying thread and wind it on the fourth body length in front of the floss. Taper it a little where it joins the floss, and make sure the thread windings are covered. If the dubbing will not adhere properly to the thread, apply a little Overton's Wonder Wax first.

4. Finish the rest of the body by applying the sections one at a time, as explained in step 3. The dubbing should not be too tight, and you must be able to pick it out a little underneath later on. Now wind the five turns of ribbing tinsel tightly forward over the body and tie it off in front. Since it is customary that the body hackle on salmon flies starts at the second turn of ribbing tinsel, it is important that this turn of tinsel falls directly in front of the hackle stem.

5. Before the hackle is wound, it must be doubled so that the fibers will sit in a back-slanted fashion. To do this, hold the hackle at a right angle above the fly body. Moisten your fingers a little with your tongue, or dip them in your martini; then stroke the fibers back continuously until all the fibers appear to be coming from one side of the stem.

6. Spiral the hackle forward over the body, taking each turn right up behind the ribbing tinsel. The fibers are constantly being stroked back as the hackle is being wound. Take a couple of extra turns close together in front, midway between the hook eye and the front of the body (the space reserved for the head). Divide that hackle evenly on top and pull a half down under the shank on each side. Hold the hackle underneath while winding the tying thread back in front of the body, binding down the base of the hackle fibers in the process. That part of the hackle is now tied under as part of the throat, which is applied next.

7. There are two methods by which the throat hackle can be applied. The first is by the "false hackle" method explained in chapter 3. The other is by winding it as a collar, such as on a hair wing (see chapter 6), and then dividing the fibers on top and tying them under as a throat, like the front of the body hackle shown in step 6. Choose a fairly webby saddle or hen neck hackle with fibers that are just slightly longer than the front of the body hackle. The consistency of the hackle can perhaps best be compared with that of a guinea fowl body feather. Make sure the room for the head is not lost when dressing the throat.

Now pick out the seal's fur body—underneath only—using a thin dubbing needle. The longest fur should be in front; then it should gradually taper down. As you pick the fur out, be careful not to break the hackle stem on the body. The finished throat can best be seen in step 10.

TYING IN THE WING

Before we go any further, I must offer some words of advice about the selection of whole feathers for wings. Unlike quill strips that can be humped and stroked into attaining the right curvature, whole feathers, such as tippets and jungle cock feathers and hackles cannot. They must be picked from opposite sides of whole necks, saddle patches, and body skins, whatever the case may be, so that the curve in the stems will match when tied in on opposite sides of the hook. In this case then, the feathers from the left side of the skin are tied in on the left side (far side) of the fly, and those from the opposite side are tied in on the right side. This holds true also when feathers are placed back to back and tied in together. This may sound like a lot of trouble and expense, but I can assure you that the result will be rewarding.

8. Select two pheasant tippet feathers of the same size and place them together, one on top of the other, with the good sides up and the tips aligned. Be sure you recognize which is left and right. I measure the length of both feathers at the same time by holding them over the body with the tips at the middle of the tail. Now stroke down the fibers at the base until the lowest ones are lined up at the tie-in spot. Trim off all the unwanted fibers, on both sides of the stem, below that point with your scissors. Leave some small stumps on the stems to aid in holding the feathers in place when tied in. They should now look as shown in step 9.

9. Nick and bend the stems at an angle close to the lowest fibers, as shown in the photograph. By doing so they are easier to handle when being tied in.

10. The feathers are now placed back to
back with the best sides out and the tips
aligned. Remember that the right side
feather forms the right wing, etc. Hold
them with your fingers close to the base of
the wing and flatten the stems with your
thumbnail. Now tie in the wing on edge,
with the feathers still held back to back.
Take two complete turns of thread and
tighten them with an upward pull as described in chapter 3, step 9, "Preparing
and Tying in the Tail." Follow with four or
five more turns applied to the right of the
first ones so the stems are securely fastened.
Make sure the stems are sitting side by side,
or it will be nearly impossible to set the
wing. Cut the surplus stems while holding
the wing and apply a drop of cement on
the windings. At this point I usually moisten my fingers a little and stroke the fibers
into shape, so the wing attains a fairly low
profile. If you have trouble in getting the
feathers to sit the way they should, try
reversing the tying thread.

11. The veilings are now prepared from two orange-dyed hackles taken from opposite sides of a whole neck. They should be wide enough to almost cover the tipped wing, and long enough to reach from the tie-in spot past the wing tip to just inside the tail. Trim the stems in the same way as the tippets.

12. Place a hackle on each side and hold them flat against the wing tippets while securing them both at the same time with several tight thread windings. Make sure the stems are lying next to those of the tippets before cutting the surplus.

13. For the sides one should cut a fairly wide strip of barred woodduck from each of the two feathers. I use the wing divider shown in chapter 1 to separate the sections to be sure they are the same size. The strip to the left in the photograph is for the right (near) wing, and the other for the left. In addition to the two side feathers, two smaller feathers are illustrated. They are the kingfisher feathers that are used as cheeks and placed on the side feathers after they are tied in.

14. Hump the feather strips gently so they attain a slight downward curve (see chapter 3), and tie in a strip on each side of the wing. They should occupy the center and extend down the wing to above the front of the lilac floss. When tying in the feathers on the left (far) side, it is advantageous to turn the vise head. Next, tie in a kingfisher cheek on each side. They should be about one-third the length of the wood-duck strips. Secure the feathers tightly and cut the surplus ends.

15. The last items to be tied in are the topping and the horns, in that order. The golden pheasant crest feathers for the topping are prepared and tied in as explained in chapter 3. When several toppings are required in the dressing, they are prepared together and tied in together, as is the case on the Orange Parson. As always, the tip of the topping should meet the tip of the tail. The horns are single fibers from the center tail of a macaw. A fiber from the left side of the tail is tied in on the right (near) side of the fly and the other on the left. They are just slightly shorter than the wing length and tied in over the cheeks and pointing upward to the rear. They curve inward and the tips extend a little above the wing. Macaw feathers are difficult, if not impossible, to get and may be left out altogether. For those who can still obtain a few, they surely add to the attractiveness of the fly. Now wind a short, smooth head before applying several coats of clear lacquer, and the Orange Parson is finished.

PREPARING TIPPET WINGS FOR SMALL FLIES

When dressing a small fly (sizes 4, 6, 8 and 10), the tippet wings will often appear too high in relation to the rest of the dressing, because of the size of whole tippet feathers. This problem can be overcome by selecting a pair of tippets that are a little longer than those normally needed for the particular size fly you are dressing, from which appropriate size wings can be cut.

16.–17. Pull off the unwanted fibers at the base and trim out the center on both feathers. Hold the feathers together back to back with the convex sides out and stroke the fibers together, gathering and holding them with your fingers until they appear as solid feathers. They can now be tied in together, with the thread windings directly around the fibers rather than the stems. After a little practice you will learn that they can be set just as well as whole tippets.

Dressing the Ranger Wing

The wings on the Ranger patterns, the Black Ranger, the Durham Ranger, and the Silver Ranger, are just slightly different than those on the Orange Parson; they feature a pair of long jungle cock neck feathers sandwiched between the wings, with an additional pair of shorter tippets set on the outside.

The materials lists for the Rangers are on pages 126-7, 131-2, and 147-48. You may dress any of the three bodies to the point of applying the wings by using the instructions given for the Orange Parson. The silver twist in the ribbing may be left out; but if you wish, to learn this procedure, study the instructions for dressing the Jock Scott a little further ahead in this chapter now.

18. After you have dressed the body, it is best to prepare all the material for the wing. Select the feathers from opposite sides of their respective necks; then measure the feathers and trim the stems as you did when dressing the Orange Parson. The jungle cock feathers (center of photograph) should reach to just inside the tail, and the long tippets to the end of the tag, but not covering the largest eye of the jungle cock feathers. The small tippets reach up to the first black bar on the large tippets and should be the same width. Remember that the feathers from the right side of the skin form the right (near) wing, etc.

19. Place the two jungle cock feathers back to back with their best sides out, and tie them in on top of the hook with three or four thread windings. Make sure the tips are sitting just inside the tail.

20. Now tie in the four tippets. First, place a long tippet on each side of the jungle cock feathers and hold them in position while fastening both on the shank at the same time with tying thread. The tips of the feathers should reach to above the tag, and the jungle cock eyes should be fully exposed at the end. Now secure a short tippet on each side of the long ones in the same manner. The black bar in the end should reach and cover the first bar on the long tippets. Hold the wing and cut the surplus.

21. The fly is finished in the usual manner. The jungle cock sides, trimmed at the base like the rest of the feathers, should lie in the center and almost reach the first black bar on the wing.

THE COMPOSITE WINGS

Salmon flies with composite wings are divided into two groups distinguished from one another by the manner in which they are dressed. This difference in procedure however, is so slight that it is often ignored, except for flies that are used for exhibit rather than fishing. To the uninformed eye, all composite wing flies look very similar. But in order to illustrate this difference for the tier, I have chosen two well-known flies as representatives for their respective groups. The first one is a Black Doctor, which has a "mixed wing" that consists of an underwing of tippet strands with golden pheasant tail strips over them. On the outside of both is a main wing of dyed and natural-colored feather strips married in a continuous "sheath." This type of wing is tied on the hook in the same manner as explained in chapter 3, where the Blue Charm is dressed. In the old days all the feathers were often tied in at one time as a bunch without marrying the fibers, and in no apparent order. I suppose the term "mixed wing" is associated with this method of dressing.

The second fly is a Jock Scott with a "built wing." Like the first one, it also consists of many types of feathers, some of which are married like the mixed wing. The principal difference between the two lies in the way the wing is applied. The underwing on the Jock Scott and other built wing patterns are usually strips of white-tip turkey tail or whole feathers set back to back, outside of which are sheaths of other feathers applied one over the other like shingles on a roof. That is, they are always applied so that the lower portion of the one previously tied in is exposed below the one that follows.

This may all sound very complicated until you have studied the various techniques. The following instructions will bring light to some of the mysteries of composite wings, and after some practice you will find them not only fascinating, but also fairly simple to dress.

Dressing the Black Doctor

(Mixed Wing)

THREAD: Black, prewaxed 6/0
TAG: Fine oval silver tinsel and yellow floss

TAIL: Golden pheasant crest and Indian crow *(scarlet)*

BUTT: Scarlet wool or Seal-Ex dubbing

BODY: Black floss

RIBBING: Oval silver tinsel

HACKLE: Dark-claret-dyed hackle

THROAT: Speckled guinea fowl

UNDERWING: Tippet in strands, with narrow strips of golden pheasant tail over

WING: Mixed — Married strands of scarlet, blue, and yellow swan, florican bustard, peacock wing, and light-mottled turkey tail, on the outside of which are narrow married strips of teal and black-barred woodduck; narrow strips of brown mallard on each side, enveloping upper wing edge

TOPPING: Golden pheasant crest

HEAD: Scarlet wool, Seal-Ex, or red tying thread

Some of the feathers mentioned in this and other wing dressings are no longer available. The swan, for example, is substituted with dyed goose, and the peacock and bustard may be substituted with feathers as suggested in chapter 1. A simplified main wing can be dressed by merely marrying the scarlet, blue, and yellow goose strips with a broader strip of brown-mottled turkey, leaving out the hard-to-get feathers altogether.

1. It is best to use a large hook, like a size 2/0 to 3/0 for the first fly. Tie in the tag and tail first, then let the tying thread hang slightly to the left of a spot above the hook point. Now dub some shredded wool or Seal-Ex on the tying thread, just enough to form a small butt.

2. Wind the butt as shown. A whole strand of scarlet wool can be used, but it tends to create a little too much bulk since it has to be both tied in as well as tied off.

3. Now finish the body and throat as previously explained in chapter 3, exactly as for dressing the Orange Parson body. The hackle on all-floss bodies can be tied in by the second floss layer instead of with the tying thread.

PREPARING THE UNDERWING

4.   Prepare the feathers for the underwing as shown in the photograph. I do not cut off the tippet strands as is often suggested. Instead, I select a whole tippet and remove the plain fibers at the base, then trim out a triangle in the middle, leaving just enough fibers on each side of the stem (center of photograph) to form a right and left side when tied in. Make sure the feather is long enough so that the remainder of the stem is clearly free to the right of the tie-in spot, with the tips reaching to the butt.

Now cut a left and a right strip of golden pheasant tail feather, and leave a bit of stem on the end, if possible. The left strip is for the right (near) wing, and the other for the left (far) wing (see the explanation in chapter 3.). The width of the strips is about one-third hook gap. These strips should be chosen to match the size fly being dressed, so that they need not be trimmed at the stem. When they are tied in, the tips should reach almost to the end of the tail. There should be very little excess feather projecting to the right of the tie-in spot, or the strips will collapse when tied in and will probably be too stiff for the size fly being dressed. If several flies are being dressed, it is best to prepare all the underwings at one time and set them aside before proceeding.

PREPARING THE MARRIED WING STRIPS

If your tying bench is anything like mine, there is never any room to do anything. However, since marrying feathers requires some organizational procedures, I recommend that you clear the table and make plenty of room so that the feathers can be laid out. Read the material list carefully and select the feathers you need for the particular pattern to be dressed, in this case the Black Doctor. Place them on the table in front of you with the good side up and the tips pointing away from you. (Also read the instructions for "Preparing and Tying in the Wing" in chapter 3.) Make sure the fibers on the feathers are long enough for the size fly you are dressing.

Since nature has provided a convenient zipper-like system by which the individual fibers can adhere to one another and form a whole feather, it is a fairly simple matter to interlock fibers from one feather with fibers from another, *provided* they come from the same side of the quill stem. The ridges of the fibers act as a tongue and groove system, to lock the strands together. Fibers from opposite sides will not stick together at all. Therefore, as you look at the feathers you have placed on the table, all the fibers to the left of the quill stems can be married and will, in this case, form the right (near) wing, and the others will do likewise for the left (far) wing.

5. Cut all the left strips first, each consisting of three fibers; for smaller flies (sizes 4 to 10) one or two fibers will suffice. Separate them from the feather with the point of your scissors, and cut them off close to the stem to get a full fiber length. Place all the left fibers in a pile to the left on the table; then cut all the right side fibers in the same manner and place them on the right side of the table. Position a divider of some sort between them so that they don't get mixed up. Remember, those to the left are for the right wing, etc.

6. Let's start by marrying the fibers for the right wing first (left pile). They are assembled in the order by which they are mentioned in the materials list, starting below with the scarlet. Hold the scarlet strip by the tip between your thumb and first finger, with the best side toward you. Hold it there while positioning the blue strip alongside it, with their tips close together. The tip of the blue should extend a little beyond the tip of the scarlet. Marrying each strand so it extends a little beyond the one preceding it makes a neat looking wing when it is tied on the hook.

7. Now, with your other hand, lay the butt end of the blue strip down close alongside of the red, grasp both in your fingers, and hold them.

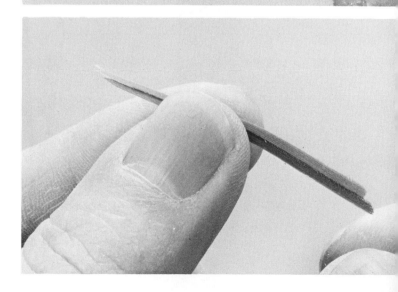

8. To marry the strips, stroke them from the butt toward the tip, moving them up and down in the process, while still holding them by the butt. When they have adhered, hold them in the middle and stroke down the butt ends as well, so that the strips are joined together for their full length.

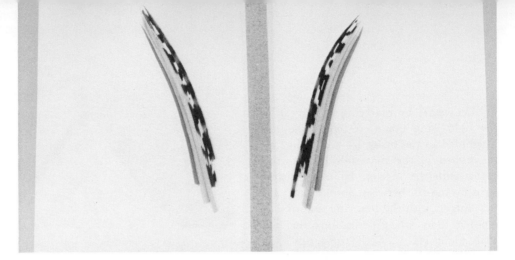

9. Add the rest of the strips, one at a time, following the preceding instructions, and the right (near) wing is finished. Now complete the left wing in the same manner except, in this case, hold the strips with the underside (dull side) toward you, unless you wish to assemble them upside down.

10. Now cut narrow strips of teal and barred woodduck long enough for the tips to reach back to above the butt when tied in, left side fibers for the right wing, etc., and marry them so that the tip of the woodduck projects a little beyond the teal (the lower strip). Their combined width should be half that of the main wing. Since only one side of the flank feathers is usable, you can strip off the other and cut the sections with a bit of stem on the end to hold the fibers together. After a while you will learn to handle these delicate feathers without the stem, but it is a convenient handle for the learner.

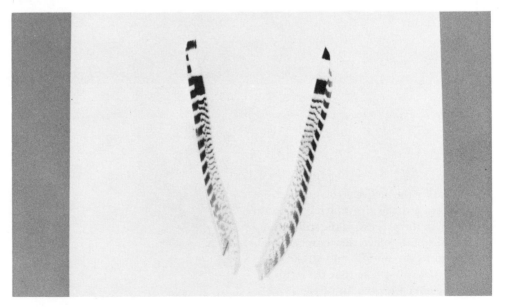

TYING IN THE WINGS

While it is perfectly acceptable to fasten the wings on fully dressed flies by the method described in chapter 3 when setting the simple strip wing, the technique I use for winging in this chapter seems to work better for the more complicated composite feather strips. The main difference between the two is that both wing strips in the following method are tied in simultaneously.

11. First stroke all the fibers on the tippet from the butt toward the tip and gather them all close together so they appear like a solid, flat feather, much as was illustrated in steps 16 and 17 in "Preparing Tippet Wings for Small Flies." Now double the feather lengthwise and tie it in as if it were two wing strips sitting back to back. The tips of the feather should reach to above the butt. Now trim the surplus and make sure the tying thread is wound to the position of the first winding applied to fasten it.

12. The two golden pheasant tail strips should now be humped as explained in chapter 3. Then the strip for the left wing is placed along the far side of the hook at the angle shown, with the tip reaching to just inside the tail. The front of the feather should be slightly down on the side of the hook at the tie-in spot. Hold it in that position with your index finger: the tip of your finger must be located exactly at the tie-in spot. While still holding the strip on the far side, place the other strip along the near side of the hook so it is lined up perfectly with the other one, and hold it in place with your thumb as shown in the next step.

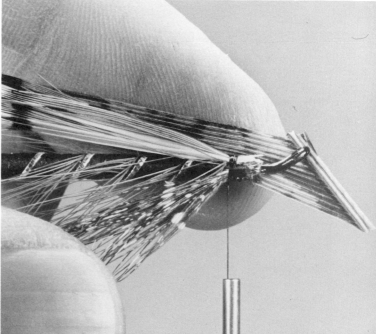

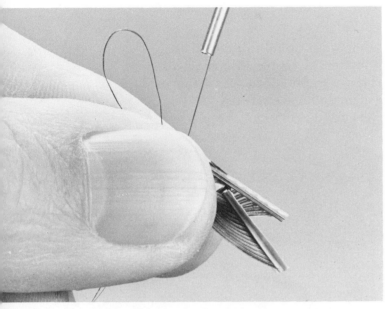

13. Position your fingertips so the upper edges of the wing strips are directly above the center of the hook shank, then bring the tying thread straight up between the near feather strip and the tip of your thumb. Hold it there while bringing the bobbin over the top and straight down between the feather strip and the fingertip on the far side—forming a small loop above the fingers in the process. Continue by again taking the thread up on the near side as before and draw the "looped" winding tight with an upward pull, thus binding the feather strips down on the hook shank. Move your fingertips back a little and take some extra turns, tightening each one with an upward pull. The wing should now sit as shown in step 14.

14. Examine the wings to make sure they are sitting correctly on both sides; then hold them in position while cutting the surplus.

15. The married main wing strips can now be tied in on each side of the underwing using the method explained in steps 12, 13, and 14. Remember, tie in the wing formed with strands from the left side of the feathers on the right (near) side, etc. Like the main wing, the married strips of teal and woodduck are humped, but are tied in on each side separately: first the right side, then the left. Position them to occupy the middle of the main wing and to reach above the butt. Trim all the surplus ends. The fly should look like the one in the photograph.

TYING IN THE BROWN MALLARD STRIPS

Many fly dressers refer to the two wing strips as the "roof" of the fly. My experience is that they are also the most difficult to set properly. When I studied with the late Bill Blades many years ago, I noted that even he had a great deal of difficulty in getting them to sit the way he intended all the time. I have since learned a method by which they can be tied in with less frustration and better results.

16. Select two brown (bronze) mallard feathers from opposite sides of the bird. They should have the same general curvature and have fibers long enough for the tips to reach the end of the wing when tied in. (On flies larger than size 1/0 they may be a little shorter, due to lack of feathers that are long enough.) Strip off the side of the feathers that is not being used, and separate a strip on each feather that is about as wide as two-thirds of the main wing. Stroke the fibers out so that they sit at a right angle to the stem.

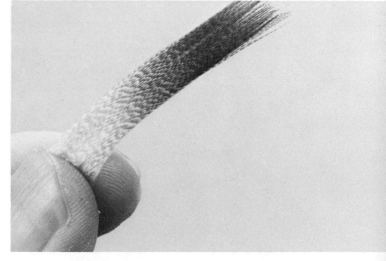

17. Cut off the segments, leaving a little stem in the end, and position one exactly on top of the other, thereby producing a double wing section. Stroke them together a little while holding them by the end of the stem.

18. Trim off the stems and hold the strip flat on top of the wing. Now fold it down over the wing so that there is a half strip on each side, thus enveloping the top. Hold it in that position while fastening it in front with tying thread. Check to see if the sections are the same size on each side. If not, take it off and do it over, remembering to tighten the thread windings with an upward pull.

19. Tie in the topping and finish off the black thread with a whip finish before cutting it. Now attach the red tying thread and wind the complete head. If you have decided to use wool for the head, it is not necessary to change thread. In that case, the wool is dubbed on the thread in the same manner as the red butt. Wool heads usually occupy only the half closest to the wing; the front half of the head is made with tying thread.

Dressing the Jock Scott

(Built Wing)

THREAD:	Black, prewaxed 6/0
TAG:	Fine oval silver tinsel and yellow floss
TAIL:	Golden pheasant crest and Indian crow
BUTT:	Black ostrich herl
BODY:	Rear half, golden yellow floss veiled above and below with toucan feathers and butted with black ostrich herl; front half, black floss
RIBBING:	Fine oval silver tinsel over rear half, wider round and flat silver tinsel over front half (On smaller flies the flat tinsel is left out; wider oval tinsel is used.)
HACKLE:	Black, palmered over black floss only
THROAT:	Speckled guinea fowl
UNDERWING:	Two strips of white-tipped turkey tail set back to back, with two strands of peacock sword tied over upper edge
WING:	Built married strands of peacock wing; yellow, scarlet, and blue swan; speckled bustard, florican bustard, and golden pheasant tail, on the outside of which are narrow married strips of teal and black-barred woodduck; wide strips of brown mallard each side, enveloping the upper edge as a sheath
SIDES:	Jungle cock
CHEEKS:	Blue chatterer
TOPPING:	Golden pheasant crest
HORNS:	Blue and yellow macaw
HEAD:	Black tying thread

Some feathers, notably the horns, cheeks, and sides, may be substituted as suggested in chapter 1, or simply left out.

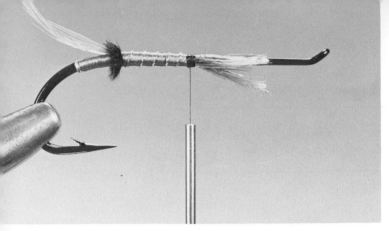

1. Tie in the tag, tail, butt, and rear body portion in the usual manner. Take five turns of ribbing over the floss body and let the tying thread hang directly in front. You are now ready for tying in the veilings, which previously have not been illustrated.

2. The delicate golden orange toucan breast feathers that are normally used for these veilings are no longer available, and I have chosen two small white feathers from the neck of a common ringneck pheasant and dyed them golden orange, as explained under "Dyes and Dyeing" in Chapter 1. They should be long enough for the tips to reach and overlap the black herl butt just slightly. Strip off the fuzz at the base and stroke the fibers together a little. The two feathers to the right in the photograph are thus prepared and ready to be tied in.

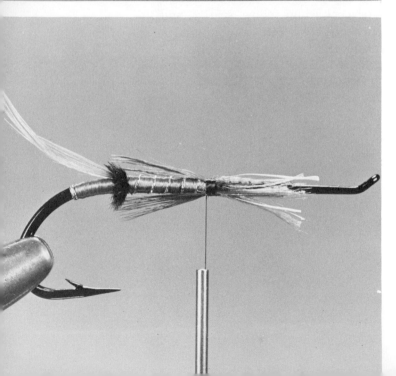

3. Tie in the feathers above and below as shown. Try to keep the feathers fairly flat and expanded to cover only the width of the body. This can be done by holding the fibers bunched together while drawing the stem slightly toward the front after fastening it loosely with thread windings. The stems are not trimmed; instead they are tied down as part of an underbody.

4. Now form the second black ostrich herl butt in front of the rear body half. Make sure the thread windings from the veilings are covered by the butt; then finish the rest of the body. Tie in the hackle. If you chose to use two tinsels for ribbing in the front body half, the round is tied in first so that it sits on the lower far side of the shank; the flat tinsel is fastened directly in the middle underneath. Take three or four turns of flat tinsel first, then follow with the round closely behind and up against the flat. Since the hackle is palmered over the front body half only, it should be chosen so that the shortest fibers are the same measure or slightly longer than the hook gap.

When the body is finished, cut a strip from the left and right side of a white-tipped turkey tail. They should be as wide as half a hook gap and be long enough to reach about the middle of the tail when tied in. (On smaller flies, the shorter, softer rump feather is used.) One of the recognizable features of a built wing is that each batch of feathers tied in does not entirely cover the ones preceding them; an ample portion of the preceding feather should be visible below. The white-tipped turkey strips must therefore sit very low and almost horizontal, to allow for the feathers to follow. This can best be accomplished by using the right strip for the right (near) wing, etc.

Place the two strips back to back with their best sides out, without humping them, reverse the thread, and tie them in on top of the hook. Trim the surplus and reverse the tying thread back to the normal clockwise direction. Now tie in the two peacock sword fibers so they follow the upper edge of the wing strips, reaching to the tip.

5. Assemble the main wing strips carefully as before and tie them in by using the instructions for the simple strip wing and the Black Doctor. Make sure the upper edges meet on top like a roof and that the white-tipped turkey tail strips are still visible below. The tips of the main wing strips should extend a little beyond the white-tipped underwing.

6. Finish the fly in the usual manner. The brown mallard in this case should be a little wider than on the Black Doctor.

SSED

the dressings are no
sted in chapter 1. In
rns. For fishing pur-
ctive tied in the hair-
er 6.

and blue chatterer

nd below with Indian
rl; front half, black

s

ay)

WING:	Mixed — Married strands of scarlet, blue, and yellow swan, florican bustard, speckled bustard, gray turkey tail, and golden pheasant tail, on the outside of which are married narrow strips of teal and barred woodduck; narrow strips of brown mallard each side enveloping the upper edge
SIDES:	Jungle cock
CHEEKS:	Blue chatterer
TOPPING:	Golden pheasant crest
HORNS:	Blue and yellow macaw
HEAD:	Black tying thread

Beauty Snow Fly

(Herl Wing)

THREAD: Black, prewaxed 6/0

BODY: Pale blue seal's fur or Seal-Ex dubbing dressed rather slim

RIBBING: Wide flat silver tinsel and gold twist (round tinsel)

HACKLE: Black heron hackle from third turn of tinsel with tips extending back to hook bend

WING: Good size bunch of peacock herl in strands

HEAD: Orange seal's fur, rather heavy and picked out so fur blends down, encircling wing and hackle for about a quarter inch

This beautiful fly is not really a fully dressed pattern, but by tradition it is always included in the classic register. It makes a fascinating fly for mounting in a frame when dressed in very large sizes.

Benchill

(Whole Feather Wing)

THREAD: Black, prewaxed 6/0

TAG: Flat gold tinsel

TAIL: Golden pheasant crest and tip of golden pheasant breast feather

BUTT: Black ostrich herl

BODY: Equal sections of orange, scarlet, and pale blue seal's fur or Seal-Ex; picked out heavy underneath

RIBBING: Flat silver tinsel and twist (round tinsel)

THROAT: Pale-blue-dyed hackle

WING: Two tippets back to back veiled with married strands of peacock wing, scarlet and blue swan, golden pheasant tail, and speckled bustard

SIDES: Fairly wide strips of speckled guinea fowl wing feather reaching to middle of wing, with jungle cock (somewhat shorter) on each side

TOPPING: Golden pheasant crest

HEAD: Black tying thread

Black Doctor

(Mixed Wing)

See tying instructions in this chapter.

Suggested Hair Wing.   A few strands of tippet and a mixed bunch of yellow, scarlet, and blue polar bear hair or dyed bucktail, over which is a main wing of fox squirrel tail; optional jungle cock on each side. The throat hackle is wound in front as a collar after the wing is tied in.

Black Dose

This and Green Highlander are the favorite flies of Richard Adams.

(Whole Feather Wing)

THREAD: Black, prewaxed 6/0

TAG: Fine oval silver tinsel and light orange floss

TAIL: Golden pheasant crest and narrow married strips of teal and scarlet swan back to back

BODY: Two turns of pale blue seal's fur, the rest black seal's fur or Seal-Ex dubbing

RIBBING: Oval silver tinsel

HACKLE: Black saddle or neck hackle

THROAT: Light-claret-dyed hackle

WING: Two tippets back to back veiled with married strands of scarlet and green swan, light-brown mottled turkey tail, and golden pheasant tail

TOPPING: Small bunch of peacock herls

HORNS: Blue and yellow macaw

HEAD: Black tying thread

Suggested Hair Wing. Hair from a black bear or bucktail dyed black with a small bunch of peacock herl tied over; jungle cock on each side. The body hackle is often left out, and instead of the claret hackle, a black hackle is wound as a collar in front after the wing is tied in.

Black Dose

(Canadian Mixed Wing)

THREAD:	Black, prewaxed 6/0
TAG:	Fine oval silver tinsel and yellow floss
TAIL:	Golden pheasant crest
BODY:	Black floss
RIBBING:	Oval silver tinsel
THROAT:	Black hackle
UNDERWING:	Two strips of black turkey (black crow for small flies)
WING:	Mixed—Married strands of red, yellow, and blue swan and golden pheasant tail, on the outside of which are fairly broad strips of gray mallard flank feather, two-thirds the wing length; narrow strips of brown mallard on each side enveloping the upper wing edge
SIDES:	Jungle cock
TOPPING:	Golden pheasant crest
HEAD:	Black tying thread

Suggested Hair Wing. Same as Black Doctor.

Black Ranger

(Whole Feather Wing)

THREAD:	Black, prewaxed 6/0
TAG:	Fine oval silver tinsel and lemon floss
TAIL:	Golden pheasant crest and Indian crow

BUTT:	Black ostrich herl
BODY:	Black floss
RIBBING:	Flat silver tinsel and twist (round tinsel)
HACKLE:	Black saddle or neck hackle
THROAT:	Deep-blue-dyed hackle
WING:	Two jungle cock feathers set back to back, veiled with two pairs of tippets (See tying instructions for whole feather wings.)
SIDES:	Jungle cock
CHEEKS:	Blue chatterer
TOPPING:	Golden pheasant crest
HORNS:	Blue and yellow macaw
HEAD:	Black tying thread

Suggested Hair Wing. Gray squirrel tail or gray fox guardhairs dyed yellow orange, set as a bunch with or without jungle cock sides and blue chatterer cheeks. The blue throat hackle is wound in front as a collar after the wing is tied in. The black body hackle is often left out on the hair-wing pattern.

Blue Doctor

(Mixed Wing)

THREAD:	Black, prewaxed 6/0
TAG:	Fine oval silver tinsel and golden yellow floss
TAIL:	Golden pheasant crest and tippet in strands
BUTT:	Scarlet wool or Seal-Ex dubbing
BODY:	Pale blue floss
RIBBING:	Oval silver tinsel
HACKLE:	Pale-blue-dyed hackle
THROAT:	Guinea fowl dyed blue (substitute for jay)

UNDERWING:

WING:

TOPPING: $\Big\}$ Same as in Black Doctor (see tying instructions.)

HEAD:

Suggested Hair Wing. Same as Black Doctor

Blue Sapphire

(Icelandic Mixed Wing)

THREAD:	Black, prewaxed 6/0
TAG:	Fine oval gold tinsel and yellow floss
TAIL:	Golden pheasant crest with red hackle fibers on one side, and blue and speckled guinea fowl fibers on the other
BODY:	Black floss, fairly heavy
RIBBING:	Oval gold tinsel
HACKLE:	Black and deep-blue-dyed hackle palmered together
THROAT:	Deep-blue-dyed hackle
UNDERWING:	Two strips of dark-brown-mottled turkey tail set back to back
WING:	Mixed—Married strips of blue-dyed goose and brown-mottled turkey tail; narrow strips of brown mallard each side enveloping upper wing edge
TOPPING:	Golden pheasant crest
HEAD:	Black tying thread

Butcher

(Built Wing)

THREAD:	Black, prewaxed 6/0
TAG:	Fine oval silver tinsel and lemon floss

TAIL:	Golden pheasant crest and blue chatterer
BUTT:	Black ostrich herl
BODY:	In four equal sections of fiery brown, pale blue, claret, and dark blue seal's fur or Seal-Ex dubbing picked out underneath
RIBBING:	Flat silver tinsel and twist (round tinsel)
HACKLE:	Dark-claret-dyed hackle
THROAT:	Lemon-dyed hackle with speckled guinea fowl in front
UNDERWING:	Two tippets back to back with golden pheasant breast feathers on each side
WING:	Built—Broad strips of teal flank feather, on the outside of which are married strands of yellow swan and speckled bustard, scarlet, blue, and orange swan, and golden pheasant tail; fairly wide strips of brown mallard on each side enveloping upper wing edge
CHEEKS:	Blue chatterer
TOPPING:	Golden pheasant crest
HORNS:	Blue and yellow macaw
HEAD:	Black tying thread

Candlestick Maker

(Whole Feather Wing)

THREAD:	Black, prewaxed 6/0
TAG:	Flat silver tinsel
TAIL:	Golden pheasant crest and strands of red swan and barred woodduck
BODY:	Rear half, black floss; front half, black seal's fur or Seal-Ex dubbing
RIBBING:	Oval silver tinsel
HACKLE:	Fiery brown hackle
THROAT:	Black hackle

WING:	Two jungle cock feathers back to back
TOPPING:	Three or four golden pheasant crests
HEAD:	Black tying thread

Childers
(Mixed Wing)

THREAD:	Black, prewaxed 6/0
TAG:	Fine oval silver tinsel and pale blue floss
TAIL:	Golden pheasant crest and Indian crow
BUTT:	Black ostrich herl
BODY:	In equal sections of golden yellow floss, orange and fiery brown seal's fur or Seal-Ex dubbing
RIBBING:	Flat silver tinsel and twist (round tinsel)
HACKLE:	Lemon-dyed badger hackle
THROAT:	Golden pheasant breast feather or crimson-dyed hackle, followed by widgeon (Substitute with teal or mallard flank.)
UNDERWING:	Two golden pheasant breast feathers back to back
WING:	Mixed — Married strands of scarlet, blue, orange, and yellow swan, speckled bustard, florican bustard, golden pheasant tail, and cinnamon and mottled gray turkey tail
SIDES:	Broad strips of barred woodduck reaching to middle of wing
CHEEKS:	Blue chatterer
TOPPING:	Golden pheasant crest
HORNS:	Blue and yellow macaw
HEAD:	Black tying thread

Dunkeld
(Mixed Wing)

| THREAD: | Black, prewaxed 6/0 |
| TAG: | Fine oval silver tinsel and light orange floss |

TAIL:	Golden pheasant crest with two jungle cock feathers back to back veiled with Indian crow feathers on each side
BUTT:	Black ostrich herl
BODY:	Flat gold tinsel
RIBBING:	Oval silver tinsel
HACKLE:	Bright-orange-dyed hackle
THROAT:	Guinea fowl dyed blue (substitute for jay)
UNDERWING:	Tippet in strands
WING:	Mixed—Married strands of scarlet, yellow, and blue swan, peacock wing, speckled bustard, florican bustard, golden pheasant tail, and mottled brown turkey tail; narrow strips of brown mallard on each side enveloping upper wing edge
SIDES:	Jungle cock
CHEEKS:	Blue chatterer
TOPPING:	Golden pheasant crest
HORNS:	Blue and yellow macaw
HEAD:	Black tying thread

Suggested Hair Wing.   A small mixed bunch of red, yellow, and blue polar bear hairs with a main wing of fox squirrel hair over; optional sides of jungle cock. The jungle cock feathers, body hackle, and throat are left out of the body, and a bright-orange-dyed hackle is wound in front as a collar after the wing is tied in.

Durham Ranger

(Whole Feather Wing)

THREAD:	Black, prewaxed 6/0
TAG:	Flat silver tinsel
TAIL:	Golden pheasant crest and Indian crow
BUTT:	Black ostrich herl
BODY:	Equal sections of lemon floss, orange, fiery brown, and black seal's fur or Seal-Ex dubbing

RIBBING: Flat silver tinsel and twist (round tinsel)

HACKLE: Badger hackle dyed yellow

THROAT: Light-blue-dyed hackle

WING:

SIDES:

CHEEKS: } Same as Black Ranger

TOPPING:

HORNS:

HEAD:

Suggested Hair Wing.   Same as Black Ranger

Dusty Miller

(Built Wing)

THREAD: Black, prewaxed 6/0

TAG: Fine oval silver tinsel and golden yellow floss

TAIL: Golden pheasant crest and Indian crow

BUTT: Black ostrich herl

BODY: Rear two-thirds, embossed silver tinsel; front third, orange floss

RIBBING: Oval silver tinsel

HACKLE: Golden-olive-dyed hackle over orange floss

THROAT: Speckled guinea fowl

UNDERWING: Two strips of white-tipped turkey tail set back to back

WING: Built — Married strands of teal, yellow, scarlet, and orange swan, speckled bustard, florican bustard, and golden pheasant tail, on the outside of which are narrow married strips of pintail or teal and barred woodduck; narrow strips of brown mallard on each side enveloping upper wing edge

SIDES: Jungle cock

TOPPING:	Golden pheasant crest
HORNS:	Blue and yellow macaw
HEAD:	Black tying thread

Suggested Hair Wing.   A small mixed bunch of yellow, scarlet, and orange polar bear hairs over which is a bunch of natural brown bucktail or fox squirrel; jungle cock sides optional. The olive-dyed hackle and speckled guinea fowl is wound in front as a collar after the wing is tied in.

(Irish Mixed Wing)

THREAD:	Black, prewaxed 6/0
TAG:	Fine oval silver tinsel and golden yellow floss
TAIL:	Golden pheasant crest and tippet in strands
BODY:	Rear quarter, bright orange seal's fur; next quarter, light blue seal's fur; rest of body, fiery brown seal's fur (Seal's fur can be substituted with Seal-Ex dubbing.)
RIBBING:	Oval silver tinsel
HACKLE:	Fiery brown over blue and fiery brown seal's fur
THROAT:	Guinea fowl dyed blue (substitute for jay)
UNDERWING:	Tippet in strands
WING:	Mixed — Married strands of scarlet, blue, yellow, and orange swan, florican bustard, speckled bustard, and golden pheasant tail, on the outside of which are married narrow strips of teal and barred woodduck; fairly broad strips of brown mallard on each side enveloping upper wing edge
HORNS:	Blue and yellow macaw
HEAD:	Black ostrich herl and tying thread

Gordon

(Mixed Wing)

THREAD:	Black, prewaxed 6/0

TAG:	Flat silver tinsel
TAIL:	Golden pheasant crest and Indian crow
BUTT:	Black ostrich herl
BODY:	Rear quarter, light orange floss; rest is ruby red floss
RIBBING:	Flat silver tinsel and twist (round tinsel)
HACKLE:	Claret-dyed hackle
THROAT:	Light-blue-dyed hackle
UNDERWING:	Two bright-red-dyed hackles back to back, with three or four peacock herls over
WING:	Mixed—Married strands of orange, scarlet, and blue swan, golden pheasant tail, and speckled bustard
CHEEKS:	Small tippet with jungle cock of same length on the outside
TOPPING:	Golden pheasant crest
HORNS:	Blue and yellow macaw
HEAD:	Black tying thread

Green Highlander

(Whole Feather Wing)

THREAD:	Black, prewaxed 6/0
TAG:	Fine oval silver tinsel and yellow floss
TAIL:	Golden pheasant crest and strip of barred woodduck
BUTT:	Black ostrich herl
BODY:	Rear quarter, yellow floss; rest, bright green seal's fur or Seal-Ex dubbing
RIBBING:	Oval silver tinsel
HACKLE:	Grass green hackle over seal's fur only
THROAT:	Bright-yellow-dyed hackle
WING:	Two tippets back to back veiled with married strands of yellow, orange, and green swan, florican bustard, peacock wing, and golden pheasant tail, on the outside of which are narrow married strips of teal and barred woodduck

SIDES:	Jungle cock
CHEEKS:	Indian crow
TOPPING:	Golden pheasant crest
HORNS:	Blue and yellow macaw
HEAD:	Black tying thread

There are many different ways of dressing the Green Highlander. The above dressing is my favorite.

Suggested Hair Wing. Tippet in strands with small bunch of yellow, orange, and green polar bear hair tied in together; natural brown bucktail hair over as a main wing with a jungle cock feather on each side. The barred wood-duck strip is omitted from the tail, but the body is dressed as usual, except that the yellow throat hackle is wound as a collar after the wing is tied in.

Helmsdale Doctor

(Mixed Wing)

THREAD:	Black, prewaxed 6/0
TAG:	Flat silver tinsel
TAIL:	Golden pheasant crest and tippet in strands
BUTT:	Scarlet wool or Seal-Ex dubbing
BODY:	Flat silver tinsel
RIBBING:	Oval silver tinsel
THROAT:	Lemon-dyed hackle
UNDERWING:	Ten to fifteen strands of peacock herl
WING:	Mixed—Married strands of scarlet, blue, orange, yellow, and white swan, cinnamon and light mottled gray turkey tail, and speckled bustard
TOPPING:	Golden pheasant crest
HEAD:	Red wool

Jock Scott

(Built Wing)

See tying instructions.

Suggested Hair Wing. A small bunch of scarlet, yellow, and blue polar bear hairs, over which is a main wing of natural brown bucktail, fairly dark. The body is kept intact as for the fully dressed pattern; the jungle cock sides for the wing are optional.

Kate

(Mixed Wing)

THREAD:	Black, prewaxed 6/0
TAG:	Fine oval silver tinsel and lemon floss
TAIL:	Golden pheasant crest and blue chatterer
BUTT:	Black ostrich herl
BODY:	Crimson floss
RIBBING:	Oval silver tinsel
HACKLE:	Crimson-dyed hackle
THROAT:	Lemon-dyed hackle
UNDERWING:	Tippet in strands
WING:	Mixed—Married strands of scarlet and yellow swan, golden pheasant tail, and speckled bustard, on the outside of which are married narrow strips of teal and barred wood-duck; narrow strips of brown mallard on each side enveloping upper wing edge
SIDES:	Jungle cock
CHEEKS:	Blue chatterer
TOPPING:	Golden pheasant crest
HORNS:	Blue and yellow macaw
HEAD:	Black tying thread

Lady Amherst

(Whole Feather Wing)

THREAD:	Black, prewaxed 6/0
TAG:	Fine oval silver tinsel and golden yellow floss
TAIL:	Golden pheasant crest and strands of teal
BUTT:	Black ostrich herl
BODY:	Flat silver tinsel
RIBBING:	Oval silver tinsel
HACKLE:	Badger
THROAT:	Teal flank feather reaching to hook barb
WING:	Two jungle cock feathers set back to back, veiled with two Amherst tippets on each side; the long tippets with square ends and the shorter ones with round ends, dressed as explained in the instructions for making the Ranger Wings
SIDES:	Jungle cock
CHEEKS:	Blue chatterer
TOPPING:	Golden pheasant crest feather
HORNS:	Blue and yellow macaw
HEAD:	Black tying thread

On small flies the tippets are substituted with strips of Amherst pheasant tail, and an underwing of Amherst tippet in strands is often used.

Lemon Grey

(Irish Mixed Wing)

THREAD:	Black, prewaxed 6/0
TAG:	Fine oval silver tinsel and golden yellow floss
TAIL:	Golden pheasant crest and Indian crow
BUTT:	Black ostrich herl
BODY:	Gray seal's fur or Seal-Ex dubbing

RIBBING:	Oval silver tinsel
HACKLE:	Grizzly
THROAT:	Lemon-dyed hackle
UNDERWING:	Tippet in strands
WING:	Mixed—Married strands of green, yellow, and orange swan, speckled bustard, florican bustard, and golden pheasant tail, on the outside of which are married narrow strips of teal and barred woodduck; fairly broad strips of brown mallard on each side enveloping upper wing edge
HEAD:	Black ostrich herl and tying thread

Mar Lodge

(Mixed Wing)

THREAD:	Black, prewaxed 6/0
TAG:	Flat silver tinsel
TAIL:	Golden pheasant crest and two jungle cock feathers back to back
BUTT:	Black ostrich herl
BODY:	Flat silver tinsel with middle fifth black floss
RIBBING:	Oval silver tinsel
THROAT:	Speckled guinea fowl
UNDERWING:	Tippet in strands
WING:	Mixed—Married strands of white, speckled bustard, florican bustard, cinnamon turkey tail, mottled gray and mottled brown turkey tail, and golden pheasant tail, on the outside of which are broad strips of barred woodduck
SIDES:	Jungle cock
TOPPING:	Golden pheasant crest
HORNS:	Blue and yellow macaw
HEAD:	Black tying thread

The black segment in the middle of the body can be made with tying thread wound over a solid silver body. This is not only simpler, but also neater looking.

Martinez Special

(Whole Feather Wing)

THREAD:	Black, prewaxed 6/0
TAG:	Fine oval gold tinsel and yellow floss
TAIL:	Golden pheasant crest with two small jungle cock feathers set back to back
BUTT:	Red wool or Seal-Ex dubbing
BODY:	Rear three-fourths, flat gold tinsel; front fourth, pale yellow green chenille
RIBBING:	Oval gold tinsel
THROAT:	Claret-dyed hackle fronted with speckled guinea fowl
WING:	Two golden pheasant tippets set back to back, on each side of which are married strands of yellow, red, and green swan, outside of which, and covering the wing, are broad married strips of teal flank and brown mallard
SIDES:	Jungle cock
CHEEKS:	Blue kingfisher
TOPPING:	Golden pheasant crest
HORNS:	Blue and yellow macaw
HEAD:	Black tying thread

Narcea River

(Whole Feather Wing)

THREAD:	Black, prewaxed 6/0
TAG:	Fine oval silver tinsel and yellow floss
TAIL:	Golden pheasant crest and Indian crow
BUTT:	Peacock herl
BODY:	Rear half, bright green chenille ribbed with fine yellow chenille, veiled below with a golden pheasant crest feather

pointing down, reaching to the hook point, and butted with peacock herl; front half, crimson seal's fur or Seal-Ex dubbing

RIBBING: Oval silver tinsel over front body half

THROAT: Speckled guinea fowl

WING: Two jungle cock feathers set back to back, on each side of which is a golden pheasant tippet, on the outside of which are married strands of yellow, green, and red swan, veiled on each side with woodduck flank covering the wing, on each side of which is a broad strip of teal flank, set low; all materials reach to above hook barb but do not cover the tip portion of the jungle cock.

SIDES: Jungle cock

CHEEKS: Blue kingfisher

TOPPING: Golden pheasant crest

HORNS: Blue and yellow macaw

HEAD: Red tying thread with black center band

Nipisiquit

(Mixed Wing)

THREAD: Black, prewaxed 6/0

TAG: Fine oval silver tinsel and yellow floss

TAIL: Golden pheasant crest and a few strands of black-barred woodduck

BUTT: Black wool, dressed sparse and thin

BODY: Gray fox underfur

RIBBING: Oval silver tinsel

HACKLE: Pale grizzly hackle palmered from third turn of tinsel

THROAT: Pale grizzly hackle, dressed sparse

UNDERWING: Tippet in strands and strips of brown-mottled turkey tail

WING: Mixed — Married strands of blue swan, Amherst pheasant tail, teal flank and brown mottled turkey, on the outside of which is a strip of black-barred woodduck, one-third as wide as the wing; fairly broad strips of brown mallard on each side enveloping upper wing edge

SIDES:	Jungle cock
TOPPING:	Golden pheasant crest
HEAD:	Black tying thread

Popham

(Mixed Wing)

THREAD:	Black, prewaxed 6/0
TAG:	Flat silver tinsel
TAIL:	Golden pheasant crest and Indian crow
BUTT:	Black ostrich herl
BODY:	In three equal sections; rear portion, orange; middle portion, lemon yellow floss, veiled above and below with Indian crow and butted with black ostrich herl; front portion, pale blue floss veiled above and below with Indian crow only
RIBBING:	Oval gold tinsel over rear and middle sections, oval silver tinsel over front section
THROAT:	Guinea fowl dyed blue (substitute for jay)
UNDERWING:	Tippet in strands
WING:	Mixed—Married strands of speckled bustard, florican bustard, peacock wing, scarlet, blue, orange, and yellow swan, and golden pheasant tail, over which are three or four strands of peacock sword fibers
SIDES:	Broad strips of barred woodduck
TOPPING:	Golden pheasant crest
HORNS:	Blue and yellow macaw
HEAD:	Black tying thread

Prince Philip

(Built Wing)

THREAD:	Black, prewaxed 6/0
TAG:	Fine oval gold tinsel and light blue floss
TAIL:	Golden pheasant crest and narrow strips of light blue and red swan
BUTT:	White ostrich herl
BODY:	Purple floss or Seal-Ex dubbing
RIBBING:	Flat gold tinsel and gold twist (round tinsel)
HACKLE:	Claret-dyed hackle over front body half
THROAT:	Magenta-dyed hackle fronted by dyed light blue hackle
UNDERWING:	Two strips of brown mottled, white-tipped turkey tail set back to back
WING:	Built—Married broad strips of blue and black swan, over which are broad strips of Amherst pheasant tail with a little narrower strips of brown mottled turkey tail or brown mallard almost as long set in middle of each side
SIDES:	Jungle cock, one-third the wing length
CHEEKS:	Blue chatterer
TOPPING:	Golden pheasant crest
HEAD:	Black tying thread

Red Sandy

(Whole Feather Wing)

THREAD:	Black, prewaxed 6/0
TAG:	Silver twist (round silver tinsel) or flat silver tinsel
TAIL:	Golden pheasant crest and Indian crow
BUTT:	Scarlet wool or Seal-Ex dubbing

BODY: Rear half, oval silver tinsel veiled above and below with Indian crow and butted with scarlet wool or Seal-Ex; front half, oval silver tinsel

RIBBING: None

HACKLE: Scarlet-dyed hackle over front body half only

THROAT: Scarlet-dyed hackle wound heavy as a collar after wing is tied in

WING: Two jungle cock feathers back to back, veiled with two Indian crow feathers (or scarlet-dyed hackle as substitute) on each side

TOPPING: Two golden pheasant crest feathers

HORNS: Red macaw

HEAD: Scarlet wool or Seal-Ex dubbing

Rosy Dawn

(Whole Feather Wing)

THREAD: Black, prewaxed 6/0

TAG: Flat gold tinsel

TAIL: Golden pheasant crest and tippet in strands

BUTT: Black ostrich herl

BODY: Rear half, embossed silver tinsel; front half, oval gold tinsel butted at the joint with a magenta-dyed hackle with fibers approximately as long as the hook gap

THROAT: Hackle dyed magenta, followed by a pale-blue-dyed hackle

WING: Two tippets back to back, veiled with married strands of yellow, blue, and scarlet swan and golden pheasant tail

SIDES: Jungle cock

TOPPING: Two or three golden pheasant crests

HORNS: Blue and yellow macaw

HEAD: Black tying thread

Salscraggie or Pale Torrish

(Built Wing)

THREAD:	Black, prewaxed 6/0
TAG:	Fine oval silver tinsel and golden yellow floss
TAIL:	Golden pheasant crest and red ibis
BUTT:	Black ostrich herl
BODY:	Rear half, oval silver tinsel butted with yellow-dyed hackle and black ostrich herl; front half, yellow seal's fur or Seal-Ex dubbing
RIBBING:	Oval silver tinsel over front half
THROAT:	Yellow-dyed hackle
UNDERWING:	Two strips of cinnamon turkey tail set back to back
WING:	Built — Married strands of red, yellow and blue swan, Amherst pheasant tail, gray mottled turkey tail, on the outside of which is a rather broad strip of pintail or teal; narrow strips of brown mallard on each side enveloping upper wing edge
SIDES:	Jungle cock
TOPPING:	Golden pheasant crest
HEAD:	Black tying thread

Sherbrook

(Mixed Wing)

THREAD:	Black, prewaxed 6/0
TAG:	Fine oval silver tinsel and lemon floss
TAIL:	Golden pheasant crest and Indian crow
BODY:	Rear third, pale orange floss; front two-thirds, pale blue floss

RIBBING: Oval silver tinsel

THROAT: Pale-blue-dyed hackle

UNDERWING: Tippet in strands

WING: Mixed—Married strands of yellow, white, orange, crimson, and blue swan, golden pheasant tail, florican bustard, and peacock wing, on the outside of which are married narrow strips of barred woodduck and pintail or teal; narrow strips of brown mallard on each side enveloping upper edge of wing

TOPPING: Golden pheasant crest

HORNS: Blue and yellow macaw

HEAD: Black tying thread

Silver Docter

(Mixed Wing)

THREAD: Black, prewaxed 6/0

TAG: Fine oval silver tinsel and golden yellow floss

TAIL: Golden pheasant crest and blue chatterer

BUTT: Scarlet wool or Seal-Ex dubbing

BODY: Flat silver tinsel

RIBBING: Oval silver tinsel

THROAT: Pale-blue-dyed hackle with widgeon or teal in front

UNDERWING:

WING:

TOPPING: } Same as Black Doctor (See tying instructions.)

HEAD:

Suggested Hair Wing.   Same as Black Doctor

Silver Grey

(Mixed Wing)

THREAD:	Black, prewaxed 6/0
TAG:	Fine oval silver tinsel and golden yellow floss
TAIL:	Golden pheasant crest and strands of black-barred woodduck
BUTT:	Black ostrich herl
BODY:	Flat silver tinsel
RIBBING:	Oval silver tinsel
HACKLE:	Badger hackle
THROAT:	Widgeon or teal
UNDERWING:	Tippet in strands
WING:	Mixed—Married strands of white, yellow, and green swan, speckled bustard, florican bustard, and golden pheasant tail, on the outside of which are married narrow strips of pintail or teal and black-barred woodduck; narrow strips of brown mallard on each side enveloping upper wing edge
SIDES:	Jungle cock
TOPPING:	Golden pheasant crest
HORNS:	Blue and yellow macaw
HEAD:	Black tying thread

Suggested Hair Wing. A small mixed bunch of white, yellow, and green polar bear hairs over which is a main wing of gray squirrel tail with a jungle cock on each side. The body hackle is left out, and a natural badger hackle is wound as a collar after the wing is tied in.

Silver Martinez

(Whole Feather Wing)

THREAD:	Black, prewaxed 6/0
TAG:	Fine oval silver tinsel

TAIL:	Golden pheasant crest and blue kingfisher
BUTT:	Red wool or Seal-Ex dubbing
BODY:	Flat silver tinsel
RIBBING:	Oval silver tinsel
THROAT:	Bright-green-dyed hackle fronted with speckled guinea fowl
WING:	Two jungle cock feathers set back to back, veiled on each side with golden pheasant tippets, on each side of which is a bright green hackle set on upper half reaching to just inside the tail, on the outside of which are whole lemon-colored woodduck flank feathers covering entire wing and reaching to just inside the tail
SIDES:	Jungle cock
CHEEKS:	Blue kingfisher
TOPPING:	Golden pheasant crest
HORNS:	Blue and yellow macaw
HEAD:	Black tying thread with red center band

Silver Ranger

(Whole Feather Wing)

THREAD:	Black, prewaxed 6/0
TAG:	Fine oval silver tinsel and yellow floss
TAIL:	Golden pheasant crest and Indian crow
BUTT:	Scarlet wool or Seal-Ex dubbing
BODY:	Flat silver tinsel
RIBBING:	Oval silver tinsel
HACKLE:	Scarlet-dyed hackle
THROAT:	Scarlet-dyed hackle
WING:	
SIDES:	
CHEEKS:	Same as Black Ranger
TOPPING:	

HORNS:	⎫	Same as Black Ranger
HEAD:	⎭	

Suggested Hair Wing. Same as Black Ranger.

Silver Wilkinson

(Whole Feather Wing)

THREAD:	Black, prewaxed 6/0
TAG:	Flat silver tinsel
TAIL:	Golden pheasant crest and tippet in strands
BUTT:	Scarlet wool or Seal-Ex dubbing
BODY:	Flat silver tinsel
RIBBING:	Oval silver tinsel
THROAT:	First blue, then magenta-dyed hackle
WING:	Two jungle cock feathers back to back, veiled with broad strips of red swan, on the outside of which are fairly wide strips of black-barred woodduck
SIDES:	Jungle cock
CHEEKS:	Blue chatterer
TOPPING:	Golden pheasant crest with small tippet over in front
HORNS:	Blue and yellow macaw
HEAD:	Black tying thread

Sir Conrad

(Mixed Wing)

THREAD:	Black, prewaxed 6/0
TAG:	Fine oval tinsel and yellow floss
TAIL:	Golden pheasant crest and tippet in strands
BUTT:	Black ostrich herl
BODY:	Four equal sections; rear fourth yellow floss, followed by

burnt orange, fiery brown, and black seal's fur or Seal-Ex dubbing

RIBBING: Flat silver tinsel and gold lace

HACKLE: Burnt-orange-dyed hackle from second turn of tinsel

THROAT: Speckled guinea fowl

UNDERWING: Fairly heavy bunch of soft hair from a brown or black bear

WING: Mixed — Married strands of orange, yellow, red, yellow, and blue swan or goose, florican bustard, and speckled bustard, on the outside of which is a narrow strip of speckled bustard married to a broad strip of black-barred woodduck reaching to middle of tag

CHEEKS: Blue kingfisher

TOPPING: Two golden pheasant crests

HORNS: Orange macaw

HEAD: Black tying thread

This fly was designed by the author for actor William "Cannon" Conrad. It was dressed on a size 7/0 10K gold-plated hook as ordered by The American Sportsman of ABC Television, who presented it framed as a gift to the actor.

Sir Herbert

(Whole Feather Wing)

THREAD: Black, prewaxed 6/0

TAG: Fine oval silver tinsel and pale orange floss

TAIL: Golden pheasant crest and Indian crow

BUTT: Peacock sword herl

BODY: Rear three-fourths, flat gold tinsel; rest, scarlet seal's fur or Seal-Ex dubbing

RIBBING: Oval silver tinsel

HACKLE: Light-orange-dyed hackle

THROAT: Golden pheasant breast feather (a crimson-dyed hackle on smaller flies)

WING:	Two tippets back to back veiled with married strands of florican bustard, blue and crimson swan, light mottled turkey tail, and golden pheasant tail, on top of which are two strands of peacock herl on each side
SIDES:	Jungle cock
TOPPING:	Golden pheasant crest
HORNS:	Scarlet macaw
HEAD:	Peacock herl

To tie the herl head you should first cover all material ends with a thin layer of tying thread; then tie in the herl near the hook eye. The herl is now wound back to the wing butts and tied off.

Fully dressed patterns: (top row) Sir Conrad, Childers; (bottom row) Popham, Green Highlander.

Sir Richard

(Mixed Wing)

THREAD:	Black, prewaxed 6/0
TAG:	Fine oval silver tinsel and dark orange floss
TAIL:	Golden pheasant crest and Indian crow
BUTT:	Black ostrich herl
BODY:	Black floss
RIBBING:	Flat silver tinsel and twist (round tinsel)
HACKLE:	Black hackle
THROAT:	Speckled guinea fowl
UNDERWING:	Tippet in strands
WING:	Mixed—Married strands of scarlet, orange, and blue swan, speckled bustard, florican bustard, mottled gray turkey tail, and golden pheasant tail, on the outside of which is a strip of guinea fowl wing feather half as wide as wing and one-third the wing length
CHEEKS:	Blue chatterer
TOPPING:	Golden pheasant crest
HORNS:	Blue and yellow macaw
HEAD:	Black tying thread

Stevenson

(Whole Feather Wing)

THREAD:	Black, prewaxed 6/0
TAG:	Fine oval silver tinsel and pale blue floss
TAIL:	Golden pheasant crest and Indian crow
BUTT:	Black ostrich herl

BODY:	Rear quarter, orange floss; front remainder, burnt orange seal's fur or Seal-Ex dubbing
RIBBING:	Flat silver tinsel and twist (round tinsel)
HACKLE:	Bright-orange-dyed hackle
THROAT:	Pale-blue-dyed hackle
WINGS:	
SIDES:	
CHEEKS:	
TOPPING:	Same as Black Ranger
HORNS:	
HEAD:	

Suggested Hair Wing.   Same as Black Ranger

Torrish

(Built Wing)

THREAD:	Black, prewaxed 6/0
TAG:	Fine oval silver tinsel and golden yellow floss
TAIL:	Golden pheasant crest and tippet in strands
BUTT:	Black ostrich herl
BODY:	Rear two-fifths, oval silver tinsel veiled above and below with Indian crow and butted with black ostrich herl; front three-fifths, oval silver tinsel
RIBBING:	Oval silver tinsel over front body portion
HACKLE:	Lemon-dyed hackle over front body portion
THROAT:	Deep-orange-dyed hackle
UNDERWING:	Two strips of white-tipped turkey tail set back to back
WING:	Built—Married strands of teal, yellow, scarlet, and orange swan, speckled bustard, florican bustard, and golden pheasant tail, on the outside of which are narrow married strips of

	pintail or teal and black-barred woodduck; narrow strips of brown mallard on each side enveloping upper wing edge
SIDES:	Jungle cock
CHEEKS:	Indian crow
TOPPING:	Golden pheasant crest
HORNS:	Blue and yellow macaw
HEAD:	Black tying thread

White Doctor

(Whole Feather Wing)

THREAD:	Black, prewaxed 6/0
TAG:	Fine oval silver tinsel and yellow floss
TAIL:	Golden pheasant crest
BUTT:	Scarlet wool or Seal-Ex dubbing
BODY:	White floss
RIBBING:	Oval silver tinsel
HACKLE:	Pale-blue-dyed hackle
THROAT:	Speckled guinea fowl dyed blue
WING:	Two golden pheasant breast feathers set back to back, on the outside of which are married strands of yellow, green, red, and blue swan, golden pheasant tail, and peacock wing; narrow strips of brown mallard on each side enveloping upper wing edge
CHEEKS:	Blue chatterer
TOPPING:	Golden pheasant crest
HORNS:	Blue and yellow macaw
HEAD:	Red wool, Seal-Ex dubbing, or red tying thread

FLIES FOR GREASED LINE FISHING

SILVER BLUE
(Hardy)

(Hardy)

"TOY A"
(Kilroy)

REDSHA...
(Original)

MARC...

LAD...

RM

...DESCENT
(...oy)

...Y C"
(...ilroy)

5

Low-Water Flies

Low-water flies were specially designed for low-water fishing during the summer months. But unlike the simple strip wings described earlier, these are dressed on special light-wire hooks (see chapter 1) where the fly occupies only half or at the most two-thirds of the shank. The advantage is that one can present the fish with a very small fly on a relatively large hook, with the bend located somewhat behind the fly itself—thus increasing the chances of hooking the short strikers.

Almost any of the orthodox fly patterns can be dressed on low-water hooks in a reduced version, but a few have become synonymous with the style. The patterns included on the list of selected low-water flies can be dressed by using the instructions set forth in the chapters dealing with simple strip wings and fully dressed salmon flies. One must bear in mind, however, that the tag should start either in the middle of the shank or two-thirds of the way down from the hook eye. The overall proportions of the fly are then regulated by the position of the tag. Since proportions are so important in this type of work, one can follow a simple guide line: If the tag starts in the middle, the tail and hackle length should be about three-quarters of a hook gap; if the tag starts two-thirds down the shank, the tail and hackle should be one hook gap long (see photographs of the two flies). The wing, of course, takes care of itself, since it always stays just inside the tip of the tail.

SELECTED LOW-WATER DRESSINGS
Blue Charm

THREAD:	Black, prewaxed 6/0
TAG:	Fine oval silver tinsel, four or five turns
TAIL:	Golden pheasant crest
BODY:	Black silk floss, fairly thin
RIBBING:	Oval silver tinsel
THROAT:	Blue-dyed hackle
WING:	Brown mottled turkey with strips of teal set on upper half
TOPPING:	Golden pheasant crest
HEAD:	Black tying thread

This fly is often dressed as a hair wing. (See Blue Charm in chapter 6.)

Claret Alder

THREAD:	Black, prewaxed 6/0
TAG:	Fine oval silver tinsel and orange floss
TAIL:	Claret wool yarn, short
BODY:	Peacock herl
RIBBING:	Oval gold tinsel
THROAT:	Dark claret hackle fibers
WING:	Brown mallard
HEAD:	Black

Green Peacock

THREAD:	Black, prewaxed 6/0
TAG:	Flat silver tinsel

TAIL:	Golden pheasant crest
BODY:	Light blue silk floss
RIBBING:	Oval silver tinsel
THROAT:	Light-blue-dyed hackle fibers
WING:	Small bunches of green peacock sword fibers
HEAD:	Black tying thread

Jeannie

THREAD:	Black, prewaxed 6/0
TAG:	Flat silver tinsel
TAIL:	Golden pheasant crest
BODY:	Rear third, lemon yellow; front two-thirds, black silk floss
RIBBING:	Oval silver tinsel
THROAT:	Black hackle fibers
WING:	Brown mallard
SIDES:	Jungle cock feathers
HEAD:	Black tying thread

Logie

THREAD:	Black, prewaxed 6/0
TAG:	Flat silver tinsel
TAIL:	Golden pheasant crest
BODY:	Rear two-fifths, pale primrose floss; remainder is ruby red floss
RIBBING:	Oval silver tinsel
THROAT:	Light-blue-dyed hackle fibers
WING:	Strips of yellow-dyed goose with broad strips of brown mallard over
HEAD:	Black tying thread

March Brown

THREAD:	Black, prewaxed 6/0
TAG:	Flat gold tinsel
TAIL:	Brown mallard fibers
BODY:	Brown Seal-Ex dubbing roughed up after ribbing is wound
RIBBING:	Oval gold tinsel
THROAT:	Fibers from brown partridge back feather
WING:	Strips of hen pheasant tail feather
HEAD:	Black tying thread

Royal Coachman

THREAD:	Black, prewaxed 6/0
TAIL:	Golden pheasant tippet in strands
BUTT:	Peacock herl
BODY:	Red floss butted in front with peacock herl
THROAT:	Natural dark reddish brown hackle fibers
WING:	Two strips of white goose
HEAD:	Black tying thread

Silver Blue

THREAD:	Black, prewaxed 6/0
TAG:	Flat silver tinsel
TAIL:	Golden pheasant tail
BODY:	Flat silver tinsel
RIBBING:	Oval silver tinsel
THROAT:	Blue-dyed hackle
WING:	Two strips of teal breast feather
HEAD:	Black tying thread

Two low-water flies. Left is a Silver Blue with the tag starting in the middle. The other is the same fly, but with the tag starting two-thirds down from the eye.

Thunder and Lightning

THREAD:	Black, prewaxed 6/0
TAG:	Oval gold tinsel and yellow floss
TAIL:	Golden pheasant crest
BODY:	Black silk floss
RIBBING:	Oval gold tinsel
HACKLE:	Orange dyed, palmered over body from second turn of tinsel
WING:	Brown mallard
TOPPING:	Golden pheasant crest
SIDES:	Jungle cock
HEAD:	Black tying thread

PÉNINSULE
DE GASPÉ
GASPÉ
PENINSULA
Gaspé Passage
PENINSULA
GASPÉ
Murdochville
Ste Anne des-Monts
Cap-Chat
LE PARC DE LA GASPÉSIE
GASPESIAN PARK
PARC DE MATANE
MATANE
PARK
PARC PETITE CASCAPEDIA
LITTLE CASCAPEDIA PARK
Grande-Vallée
Madeleine Centre
Mont-Louis
Les Méchins
CAMPBELLTON

6

Hair-Wing Flies

My first reaction to salmon flies dressed with simple wings of hair was not an enthusiastic one. They reminded me a little too much of ordinary wet flies of the sort that one uses for just ordinary trout fishing. I have made peace with myself and accepted them as an important part of a salmon angler's fly collection. Many of the old timers on the river still would not want to get caught with these "fox-smelling" things in their fly box along side the classic feather wings even though some of the most effective ones, like the Green Highlander and the Black Dose are converted feather wing ties.

The hair-winged salmon flies actually bear little resemblance to the beautiful feather wings from the days of Kelson and Pryce-Tannatt in the 1800's, but they have proven their worth in rivers throughout the world to the point that many of the old classics are now converted to hair wings. That is, the feather wing is replaced by hair that is either natural or dyed to maintain the identifying color scheme of a particular pattern; the bodies are usually kept intact.

In general, though, hair wings patterns as such have never been anything but hair wings. They were often designed in series consisting of many flies, such as the celebrated Rat series. (The name "Rat" stems not from the four-legged variety, but refers to the first series and the initials of its author, Mr. Roy Angus Thomson). If you are interested in further study of the origin of hair wings, or other historical facts pertaining to salmon flies in general, I can highly recommend Colonel Joseph D. Bates, Jr.'s classic book, *Atlantic Salmon Flies and Fishing* (Stackpole, Harrisburg, PA). It has been invaluable to me for many years.

Most hair-wing flies are easy to dress if you have mastered the tying techniques that have been previously described, with particular reference to those in chapter 1.

Dressing the Rusty Rat

THREAD:	Red, prewaxed 6/0
TAG:	Fine oval gold tinsel
TAIL:	Three or four short peacock sword fibers
BODY:	Rear half, yellow floss; front half, peacock herl
RIBBING:	*medium* Oval gold tinsel
VEILING:	Length of yellow floss over rear body half, extending to middle of tail
WING:	Gray fox guardhairs
CHEEKS:	Jungle cock eyes (optional)
HACKLE:	Grizzly wound as a collar after the wing is tied in
HEAD:	Red tying thread

It is customary to dress all the Rat patterns with red tying thread throughout, including the Rusty Rat.

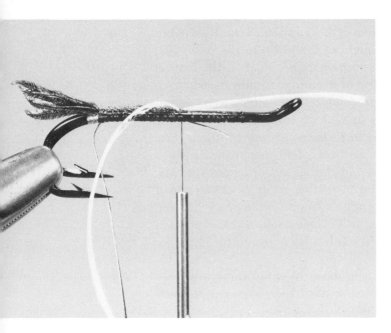

1. Tie in the fine oval gold tinsel on a size 2 double hook and form the tag as explained in chapter 3. It should occupy a space from above the hook point down to above midway between the hook point and the point of the barb.

Now tie in three or four peacock sword fibers for the tail directly in front of the tag, together with a five-inch length of oval gold ribbing tinsel somewhat heavier than for the tag. The tail should not project beyond the bend of the hook, and the tinsel is tied in under the shank.

Proceed by winding the tying thread to the middle of the hook shank, and tie in a six-inch length of yellow floss on top. Let a one-inch end of the floss extend forward over the eye of the hook for use as a veiling later.

2. Wind the yellow floss to the rear, close to the tag, so the tie-in windings for the tail and ribbing are covered. Now wind it back over the first layer to the middle of the hook shank. Before tying off, lay the short veiling material back over the body and secure it on top with a couple of turns of floss. Trim the veiling so it reaches to about the middle of the tail.

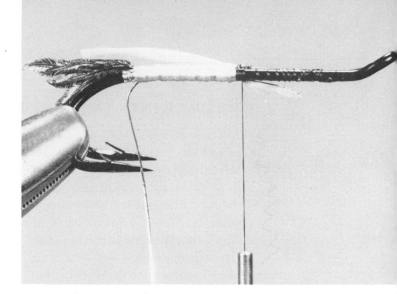

3. Tie in three or four medium-heavy peacock herls directly in front of the yellow body portion, and form a double piece of thread, as you would for a spun dubbing loop, that is a little longer than the herls. Twist the thread together to form a single heavy strand. The thread will add strength to the otherwise fragile herl and prevent them from being torn by the first fish. Move the bobbin forward, binding down the herls.

4. Twist the herl and the thread lightly together, much as if you were making a spun dubbing loop, and wind it on the front portion of the shank. Tie it off in front and trim the surplus. Make sure there is space left in front for the wing and hackle. Now spiral the oval gold ribbing forward over the entire body, five or six turns. Tie it off at the same place as the herl and trim the surplus. This finishes the body, and you are ready to prepare the wing.

PREPARING AND TYING IN THE HAIR WING

There seems to be a popular misconception about hair wings as they relate to salmon flies, and I would like to first clarify a few points of importance before proceeding to the ties. While it is customary to align the tips of the hair in a "tamping" device when dressing certain trout flies, such practice should definitely be avoided when preparing the hair wing for a salmon fly. It gives your fly the well-known "paint brush" look that totally ruins its appearance. The hair will be sufficiently aligned all by itself if it is held out from the skin or tail at a right angle before it is cut off (see step 5). After cutting the hair, it's rarely necessary to do anything but remove the short hairs and fuzz at the base.

5. For the wing on the Rusty Rat I have selected a clean piece of skin from the back of a gray fox. Make sure the hair is long enough for the size fly you are tying, at least as long as the hook. Gather up a bunch of hair between your fingers and hold them out at a right angle before cutting them off close to the skin. Now remove any long hairs that might stick out in the end of the main bunch. When tying very small flies, the best hair is found around the neck and face area of the fox.

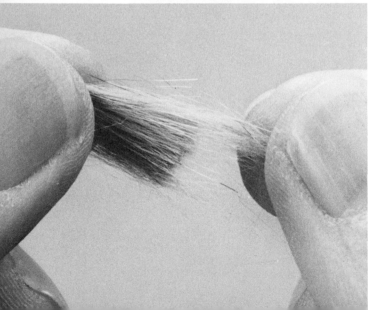

6. Since guard hairs are very thin, I pull out only a little more than half of the underfur. The rest is left in the bunch to hold the fibers together and make a more opaque wing.

7. Measure the wing length by holding the hair as shown in the photograph. The tip of the wing should reach to the end of the tail when held at the spot where it is to be tied in.

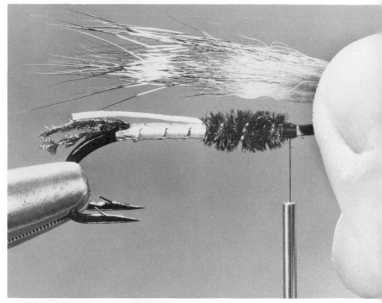

8. Now grasp the hair with your other hand, close against the fingers that previously held it. Trim away the butt ends directly across, close to your fingertips.

9. Apply a little cement on the butt ends and tie in the wing with four or five tight turns of thread. Again, make sure that there is room in front for the hackle and a small head, and that all the hair sits on top of the shank.

TYING IN THE
HACKLE COLLAR

10. Since a soft hen or webby saddle hackle is desirable for the collar, hackle selection is simplified and the supply is almost unlimited. What remains to be determined, then, is how to pick the proper size. Select a hackle and stroke it down the center stem until the fibers stand out at an angle. The fibers in the middle third of the hackle should be a hook gap and a half in length, on the average. Cut away the tip portion and trim off the fibers on each side, one-half inch up the stem, with your scissors. Leave some short stumps to prevent it from slipping when it's tied in.

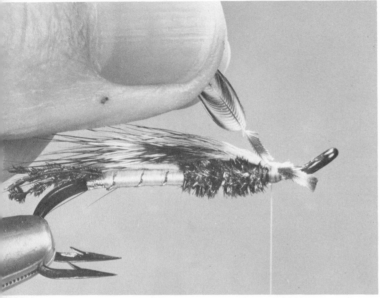

11. With the best side up, hold back the first fibers with your fingers and tie in the hackle in front of the wing with three or four tight turns of tying thread. Leave a small portion of stem between the lowest fibers and the tie-in winding to insure a good start when doubling and winding the hackle. Trim away the surplus stem.

12. Moisten your fingers a little and stroke the fibers back so they all appear to be coming from one side of the stem.

13. Now apply three or four turns of hackle, holding the fibers doubled back at the start of each turn. Tie off the hackle with several tight turns of thread, then cut the surplus.

14. Hold the fibers back with your fingers and wind the head. I sometimes wind a little back on the hackle to give it a slanted-back position. Apply some cement on the head, and your fly is finished.

Dressing the Blue Rat

I am occasionally obliged to design a salmon fly for a special occasion or specific area of fishing. This may seem totally unnecessary in view of the array of flies that already seem to cover the spectrum of colors and materials from one end to the other. But if there is something a salmon angler or fly dresser can't stand, it's one fly taking all the glory. One good pattern simply doesn't take up enough space in the fly box, which at all costs must be stuffed full to overflowing.

The Blue Rat is intended specifically for fishing in Iceland, where flies with blue seem to take more fish than others. My good friend, Joe Bates, Jr., fished them for the first time on a recent trip to Laxa i Kjos and Nordura in Iceland with great success. "An outstanding fly," he said, "as good as the Blue Charm, which is usually the best."

HOOK:	Double, sizes 2 to 12 (for Iceland)
THREAD:	Red, prewaxed 6/0
TAG:	Fine oval gold tinsel
TAIL:	Four short peacock sword fibers
BODY:	Rear half, silver doctor blue floss; front, peacock herl
RIBBING:	Oval gold tinsel
VEILING:	Length of blue floss over rear body half
WING:	Gray fox guardhair
CHEEKS:	Jungle cock eyes and blue kingfisher (or substitute)
HACKLE:	A small bunch of grizzly hackle fibers tied over the wing, with a similar bunch tied in as a throat, both well spread out
HEAD:	Red tying thread

The fly works just as well if the jungle cock and kingfisher are left out; instead I tie in a hen neck feather dyed kingfisher blue extending one-third down each side of the wing, and wind the hackle as a collar.

15. Dress the body and wing in the same manner as the Rusty Rat, but use the blue floss. Then tie in a jungle cock nail on each side reaching to the middle of the wing, on the outside of which is a blue kingfisher feather about half as long as the jungle cock.

16. Now tie in a grizzly "false hackle" throat as previously explained in chapter 3, and a similar bunch of fibers of the same length on top of the wing. The grizzly fibers are allowed to expand around the front up to, but not covering, the cheeks above or below. After the head is wound and lacquered, the Blue Rat is finished.

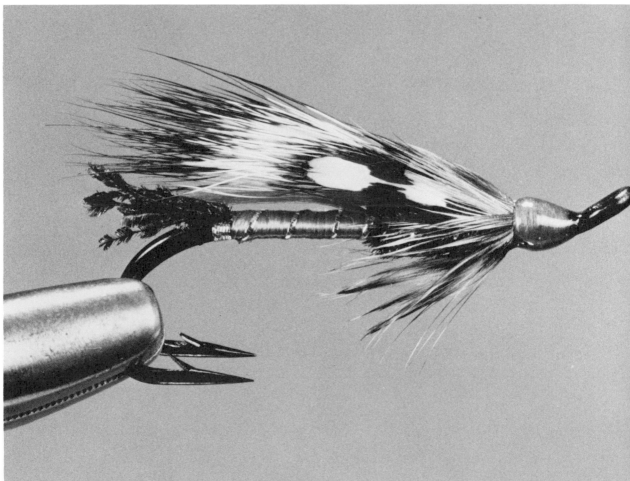

SELECTED HAIR-WING PATTERNS

In addition to the dressings listed on the following pages, suggested hair-wing schemes have been designed for many of the classic fully dressed flies. They are listed together with the traditional dressings in chapter 4. Included there are hair wings for the following flies: Akroyd, Blue Doctor, Black Dose, Black Doctor, Black Ranger, Durham Ranger, Dunkeld, Dusty Miller, Green Highlander, Jock Scott, Silver Doctor, Silver Grey, Silver Ranger, and Stevenson.

Arndilly Fancy

THREAD:	Black, prewaxed 6/0
TAG:	Fine oval silver tinsel
TAIL:	Golden pheasant crest
BODY:	Yellow floss
RIBBING:	Oval silver tinsel
THROAT:	Bright-blue-dyed hackle
WING:	Dark blackish brown fitchtail
HEAD:	Black tying thread with red band close to wing

Atherton Squirrel Tail

THREAD:	Black, prewaxed 6/0
TAG:	Flat silver tinsel
TAIL:	Golden pheasant crest
BODY:	Black Seal-Ex dubbing
RIBBING:	Oval silver tinsel
THROAT:	Fiery brown hackle
WING:	Fox squirrel tail
HEAD:	Black tying thread

Black Bear

THREAD:	Black, prewaxed 6/0
TAIL:	Two narrow sections of black crow wing quill
BODY:	Black wool or Seal-Ex dubbing
THROAT:	Small bunch of black bear hair extending to hook bend, dressed sparse
WING:	Bunch of black bear hair reaching to end of tail
HEAD:	Black tying thread

Black Bomber

THREAD:	Black, prewaxed 6/0
TAG:	Fine oval silver tinsel and yellow floss
TAIL:	Golden pheasant crest
BODY:	Black wool or Seal-Ex dubbing
RIBBING:	Oval silver tinsel
THROAT:	Black hackle
WING:	Black squirrel or black bear hair
SIDES:	Jungle cock
TOPPING:	Golden pheasant crest
HEAD:	Black tying thread

Black Cosseboom

THREAD:	Red, prewaxed 6/0
TAG:	Embossed silver tinsel
TAIL:	Black floss, one and a half hook gaps long
BODY:	Black floss or Seal-Ex dubbing
RIBBING:	Embossed silver tinsel

WING:	Gray squirrel tail with four or five peacock sword fibers over, both extending to hook bend
SIDES:	Jungle cock
HACKLE:	Black hackle wound as a collar and tied back to blend with wing
HEAD:	Black tying thread

Black Fitchtail

THREAD:	Black, prewaxed 6/0
TAG:	Fine oval silver tinsel and golden yellow floss (Yellowish orange fluorescent floss may be used, in which case it should be lacquered.)
TAIL:	Golden pheasant crest
BODY:	Black floss
RIBBING:	Oval silver tinsel
THROAT:	Black hackle
WING:	Black fitchtail
HEAD:	Black tying thread

Black Jack

THREAD:	Black, prewaxed 6/0
TAG:	Fine oval silver tinsel
TAIL:	Small bunch of golden pheasant tippet in strands
BODY:	Black floss, dressed thin
RIBBING:	Oval silver tinsel
HACKLE:	Black hackle wound heavy as a collar, with fibers reaching to end of body
HEAD:	Black tying thread

Black Labrador

THREAD:	Black, prewaxed 6/0
TAIL:	Heavy bunch of black bear hair or dyed calf tail, one body length
BODY:	Black Seal-Ex dubbing or wool dressed heavy and cigar shaped
HACKLE:	Black hackle wound as a collar with fibers extending to the hook point
HEAD:	Black tying thread

Black Rat

THREAD:	Red, prewaxed 6/0
TAG:	Fine oval silver tinsel
TAIL:	Small golden pheasant crest
BODY:	Black seal's fur or Seal-Ex dubbing
RIBBING:	Oval silver tinsel (or flat)
WING:	Gray fox guardhair
SIDES:	Jungle cock
HACKLE:	Grizzly hackle wound as a collar and tied back to blend with wing
HEAD:	Red tying thread

Blue Charm

THREAD:	Black, prewaxed 6/0
TAG:	Fine oval silver tinsel and yellow floss
TAIL:	Golden pheasant crest
BODY:	Black floss
RIBBING:	Oval silver tinsel

THROAT:	Deep-blue-dyed hackle
WING:	Woodchuck guardhair or eastern pine squirrel
HEAD:	Black tying thread

Blue Rat

See hair-wing tying instructions.

Blue Vulture

(Dressed on Double Hook)

THREAD:	Black, prewaxed 6/0
TAG:	Fine silver wire
BODY:	Finest black fur dubbing or floss
RIBBING:	Oval silver tinsel
WING:	Small bunch of gray squirrel tail reaching to end of tag with a bunch of dark brown fitchtail, slightly longer, tied over; both materials set very low and sparse
SIDES:	Jungle cock
HACKLE:	Plain blue vulturine hackle wound as a collar and tied back to blend with the wing
HEAD:	Black tying thread with red center band

As a companion to the Blue Vulture, I dress a fly I call the "Silver Vulture." The dressing is the same except that the tag is gold wire, the body is flat silver tinsel, and the ribbing is oval gold tinsel.

Butterfly

THREAD:	Black, prewaxed 6/0
TAIL:	A good size bunch of red-dyed hackle fibers, one body length
BODY:	Bronze peacock herl or black wool

WING: White goat hair or calf tail, slightly longer than the body; hair divided into two bunches in splayed fashion, and set fairly low

HACKLE: Several turns of soft brown hackle wound dry fly style

HEAD: Black tying thread

Copper Killer

THREAD: Black, prewaxed 6/0

TAG: Fine copper wire and small segment of pale green floss

TAIL: Small bunch of golden pheasant tippet in strands

BUTT: Red wool or Seal-Ex dubbing

BODY: Flat copper tinsel

RIBBING: Copper wire

HACKLE: Hot-orange-dyed hackle wound as a collar and tied back, but not under

WING: Fox squirrel tail hair extending to end of tail

HEAD: Red tying thread

Cosseboom Special

THREAD: Black, prewaxed 6/0

TAG: Embossed silver tinsel

TAIL: Olive green floss, as long as one and a half hook gaps

BODY: Olive green floss

RIBBING: Embossed silver tinsel

WING: Gray squirrel tail reaching to hook bend

SIDES: Jungle cock

HACKLE: Lemon-dyed hackle wound as a collar and tied back to blend with the wing

HEAD: Red tying thread

Crossfield

THREAD:	Black, prewaxed 6/0
TAG:	Fine oval silver tinsel
TAIL:	Golden pheasant crest
BODY:	Embossed silver tinsel
THROAT:	Medium-blue-dyed hackle
WING:	Gray squirrel tail
HEAD:	Black tying thread

Darbee Spate Fly

THREAD:	Red, prewaxed 6/0
TAG:	Fine oval gold tinsel
TAIL:	Golden pheasant crest
BODY:	Dark fiery brown polar bear underfur, wool, seal's fur, or Seal-Ex dubbing
RIBBING:	Oval gold tinsel
THROAT:	Black hackle
WING:	Brown bucktail
SIDES:	Broad strips of black-barred woodduck, two-thirds wing length
HEAD:	Red tying thread

Englehardt Special

(Dressed on Double Low-Water Hook)

THREAD:	Black, prewaxed 6/0
TAG:	Fine oval gold tinsel starting over point of hook
BODY:	Bronze peacock herl
RIBBING:	Oval gold tinsel

THROAT:	Black hackle
WING:	Soft black bear hair reaching to hook bend
SIDES:	Jungle cock
HEAD:	Black tying thread

Frazer

THREAD:	Black, prewaxed 6/0
TAG:	Fine oval silver tinsel
TAIL:	Yellow wool, short
BODY:	Three equal sections; rear, yellow wool; middle, dark green wool; front, black wool
RIBBING:	Oval silver tinsel
WING:	First small bunch of green bucktail with small bunch of fox squirrel on top, over which is a heavier bunch of gray squirrel tail
SIDES:	Jungle cock
HACKLE:	Black hackle wound as a collar
HEAD:	Red tying thread

Garry

THREAD:	Black, prewaxed 6/0
TAG:	Fine oval silver tinsel
TAIL:	Golden pheasant crest, tippet in strands, and red ibis
BUTT:	Black ostrich herl
BODY:	Black floss
RIBBING:	Oval silver tinsel
HACKLE:	Black
THROAT:	Speckled guinea fowl dyed blue
WING:	Small bunch of red bucktail with a larger bunch of yellow bucktail over

SIDES:	Jungle cock
HEAD:	Black tying thread

Gold Rat

THREAD:	Red, prewaxed 6/0
TAG:	Fine oval silver tinsel
TAIL:	Golden pheasant crest feather dyed red
BODY:	Flat gold tinsel
RIBBING:	Oval silver tinsel
WING:	Gray fox guardhair
SIDES:	Jungle cock
HACKLE:	Grizzly hackle wound as a collar and tied back to blend with the wing
HEAD:	Red tying thread

Gold Cosseboom

THREAD:	Black, prewaxed 6/0
TAG:	Embossed silver tinsel
TAIL:	Golden pheasant crest
BODY:	Embossed gold tinsel
RIBBING:	Oval silver tinsel
WING:	Gray squirrel tail with four or five peacock sword fibers over, both reaching to hook bend
SIDES:	Jungle cock
HACKLE:	Light-blue-dyed hackle wound as a collar and tied back to blend with the wing
HEAD:	Red tying thread

Green Conrad

THREAD:	Black, prewaxed 6/0
TAG:	Fine oval gold tinsel

TAIL:	Golden pheasant crest
BUTT:	Bronze peacock herl
BODY:	Flat embossed gold tinsel
RIBBING:	Oval gold tinsel
WING:	Polar bear hair dyed bright green
TOPPING:	Golden pheasant crest
HACKLE:	Bright-green-dyed hackle wound as a collar and tied back to blend with the wing, and with the tips reaching the hook point
HEAD:	Black tying thread

Green Butt

THREAD:	Black, prewaxed 6/0
TAG:	Fine oval silver tinsel and bright green fluorescent floss, wound over white silk and lacquered
TAIL:	Golden pheasant crest
BODY:	Black floss or Seal-Ex dubbing
RIBBING:	Oval silver tinsel
THROAT:	Black hackle
WING:	Soft black bear or black squirrel hair
HEAD:	Black tying thread

This fly can also be dressed with a red butt, in which case it is called just that, the Red Butt.

Grey Rat

THREAD:	Red, prewaxed 6/0
TAG:	Fine oval silver tinsel
TAIL:	Small golden pheasant crest
BODY:	Underfur from a gray fox, or gray Seal-Ex dubbing
RIBBING:	Flat gold tinsel
WING:	Gray fox guardhair
SIDES:	Jungle cock

HACKLE:	Grizzly hackle wound as a collar and tied back to blend with the wing
HEAD:	Red tying thread

Grizzly King

THREAD:	Black, prewaxed 6/0
TAG:	Flat silver tinsel
TAIL:	Narrow strip of red-dyed goose or small bunch of red-dyed hackle fibers
BODY:	Green floss
RIBBING:	Oval silver tinsel
WING:	Gray squirrel tail hair
SIDES:	Jungle cock
HACKLE:	Grizzly hackle wound as a collar and tied back to blend with the wing
HEAD:	Black tying thread

Hairy Mary

THREAD:	Black, prewaxed 6/0
TAG:	Fine oval gold tinsel
TAIL:	Golden pheasant crest
BODY:	Black floss
RIBBING:	Oval gold tinsel
THROAT:	Bright-blue-dyed hackle
WING:	Reddish brown fitchtail or squirrel
HEAD:	Black tying thread

Lady Atherton

THREAD:	Black, prewaxed 6/0
TAG:	Fine oval silver tinsel and fluorescent orange floss, wound over white thread (silk) and lacquered

BODY: Underfur from a black bear or Seal-Ex dubbing

RIBBING: Oval silver tinsel

THROAT: Black hackle fibers, very sparse

WING: Two heavy black bear hairs extending half a hook length beyond the bend, tied flat over the body as horns, with a bunch of black bear hair over, reaching to the hook bend

CHEEKS: Jungle cock, very short

HEAD: Black tying thread

Lady Joan

THREAD: Black, prewaxed 6/0

TAG: Fine oval gold tinsel

BODY: Burnt orange wool or Seal-Ex dubbing

RIBBING: Oval gold tinsel

THROAT: Yellow-dyed hackle

WING: Small bunch of black bear hair with gray squirrel tail over

SIDES: Jungle cock

HEAD: Black tying thread

Mickey Finn

THREAD: Black, prewaxed 6/0

TAG: Fine silver wire

BODY: Flat silver tinsel

RIBBING: Oval silver tinsel

WING: In three sections; yellow bucktail, over which is a bunch of red bucktail of same size, over which is another bunch of yellow bucktail as large as the other two combined

SIDES: Jungle cock

HEAD: Black tying thread

Minktail

THREAD:	Black, prewaxed 6/0
TAG:	Fluorescent yellow floss, wound over white silk and lacquered
TAIL:	Golden pheasant crest
BODY:	Black floss
RIBBING:	Oval silver tinsel
THROAT:	Black hackle
WING:	Light brown mink or fitchtail
HEAD:	Black tying thread

Muddler Minnow

THREAD:	Black, prewaxed 6/0 (use size A or B thread for head.)
TAIL:	A double section of brown mottled turkey wing quill
BODY:	Flat gold tinsel
WING:	Small bunch of gray squirrel tail hair, on each side of which is a wide section of brown mottled turkey wing quill
COLLAR:	Natural deer body hair, two-thirds the wing length
HEAD:	Natural deer body hair spun on the hook and trimmed cone shaped

The Muddler can also be tied with a marabou wing that is black, white, or yellow, in which case the tail is most often left out, or replaced with a small bunch of marabou.

Onset

THREAD:	Black, prewaxed 6/0
TAG:	Golden pheasant crest
BODY:	Rear third, bright yellow floss; remainder, bright orange floss
RIBBING:	Oval silver tinsel

THROAT:	Medium-blue-dun hackle
WING:	Gray squirrel tail hair
HEAD:	Black tying thread

Orange Blossom

THREAD:	Black, prewaxed 6/0
TAG:	Fine oval silver tinsel and golden yellow floss
TAIL:	Golden pheasant crest and Indian crow
BUTT:	Black ostrich herl
BODY:	Embossed silver
WING:	Palest natural brown bucktail
HACKLE:	Bright-orange-dyed hackle wound as a collar and tied back to blend with the wing, tips extending to the hook point
HEAD:	Black tying thread

Orange Charm

THREAD:	Black, prewaxed 6/0
TAG:	Fine oval silver tinsel and yellowish orange fluorescent floss, wound over white silk and lacquered
TAIL:	Golden pheasant crest
BODY:	Black floss
RIBBING:	Oval silver tinsel
THROAT:	Bright-orange-dyed hackle
WING:	Woodchuck guardhair or eastern pine squirrel tail
HEAD:	Black tying thread

Orange Cosseboom

THREAD:	Black, prewaxed
TAG:	Flat gold tinsel

TAIL:	Orange floss, as long as one and a half hook gaps
BODY:	Orange floss or Seal-Ex dubbing
RIBBING:	Flat gold tinsel
WING:	Gray squirrel tail hair with four or five peacock sword fibers over, both reaching to hook bend
SIDES:	Jungle cock
HACKLE:	Black hackle wound as a collar and tied back to blend with the wing
HEAD:	Black tying thread

Pale Torrish

THREAD:	Black, prewaxed 6/0
TAG:	Fine oval silver tinsel and golden yellow floss
TAIL:	Golden pheasant crest
BUTT:	Black ostrich herl
BODY:	Flat silver tinsel
RIBBING:	Oval silver tinsel
THROAT:	Bright-yellow-dyed hackle
WING:	A small mixed bunch of scarlet, blue, and yellow polar bear hairs, over which is a small bunch of natural brown bucktail
HEAD:	Black tying thread

Peacock Cosseboom

THREAD:	Black, prewaxed 6/0
TAG:	Embossed silver tinsel
TAIL:	Four or five peacock sword fibers extending to the bend
BODY:	Rear half, embossed gold tinsel; front half, bronze peacock herl
RIBBING:	Oval silver tinsel
THROAT:	Four or five peacock sword fibers, half a body length

WING:	Gray squirrel tail hair, with four or five peacock sword fibers over, both reaching to the hook bend
SIDES:	Jungle cock
HEAD:	Red tying thread

Priest

THREAD:	White, prewaxed 6/0
TAG:	Fine oval silver tinsel
TAIL:	Small bunch of blue dun hackle fibers
BODY:	White fluorescent wool or floss
RIBBING:	Oval silver tinsel
WING:	White calf tail hair
HACKLE:	Light blue dun hackle wound as a collar and tied back to blend with the wing, tips reaching to the hook point
HEAD:	White tying thread

Professor

THREAD:	Black, prewaxed 6/0
TAG:	Fine oval gold tinsel
TAIL:	Small bunch of red-dyed hackle fibers
BODY:	Yellow floss
RIBBING:	Oval gold tinsel
WING:	Gray squirrel tail hair
HACKLE:	Soft natural brown hackle wound as a collar and tied back to blend with the wing
HEAD:	Black tying thread

Red Abbey

THREAD:	Black, prewaxed 6/0
TAG:	Fine oval silver tinsel

TAIL:	Section of red-dyed goose quill
BODY:	Red floss, wool, or Seal-Ex dubbing
RIBBING:	Oval silver tinsel
THROAT:	Brown hackle fibers
WING:	Fox squirrel tail or brown bucktail
SIDES:	Jungle cock
HEAD:	Black tying thread

Red Cosseboom

THREAD:	Black, prewaxed 6/0
TAG:	Embossed silver tinsel
TAIL:	Red floss, as long as one and a half hook gaps
BODY:	Red floss, wool, or Seal-Ex dubbing
RIBBING:	Embossed gold tinsel
WING:	Gray squirrel tail
SIDES:	Jungle cock
HACKLE:	Black hackle wound as a collar and tied back to blend with the wing
HEAD:	Red tying thread

Red Dog

THREAD:	Black, prewaxed 6/0
TAG:	Fine oval silver tinsel and golden yellow floss
TAIL:	Golden pheasant crest
BODY:	Flat silver tinsel
RIBBING:	Oval silver tinsel
HACKLE (Body):	Yellow-dyed hackle
WING:	Natural brown bucktail

HACKLE
(Collar):   Natural red hackle wound as a collar and tied back slightly

HEAD: Black tying thread

Roger's Fancy

THREAD: Black, prewaxed 6/0

TAG: Fine oval silver tinsel and fluorescent yellow floss wound over white silk and lacquered

TAIL: Three or four peacock sword fibers reaching to the bend

BODY: Bright green wool or Seal-Ex dubbing

RIBBING: Oval silver tinsel

THROAT: Bright-yellow-dyed hackle fibers fronted by bright-green-dyed hackle fibers

WING: Gray fox guard hair

SIDES: Jungle cock, fairly short

HEAD: Black tying thread

Rusty Rat

See hair-wing tying instructions.

Stoat Tail

THREAD: Black, prewaxed 6/0

TAG: Fine oval silver tinsel

TAIL: Golden pheasant crest

BODY: Black floss

RIBBING: Oval silver tinsel

THROAT: Soft black hackle fibers

WING: Hair from a black stoat tail or natural black squirrel

HEAD: Black tying thread

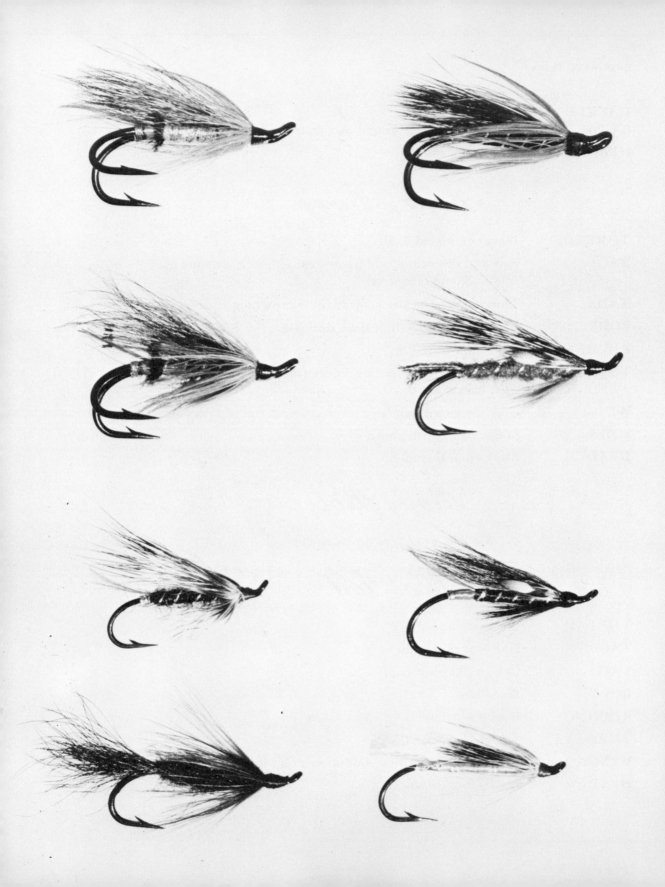

Silver Rat

THREAD:	Red, prewaxed 6/0
TAG:	Fine oval gold tinsel
TAIL:	Short golden pheasant crest
BODY:	Flat silver tinsel
RIBBING:	Oval gold tinsel
WING:	Gray fox guard hair
SIDES:	Jungle cock
HACKLE:	Grizzly hackle wound as a collar and tied back to blend with the wing
HEAD:	Red tying thread

Thunder and Lightning

THREAD:	Black, prewaxed 6/0
TAG:	Fine oval gold tinsel and claret floss
TAIL:	Golden pheasant crest
BUTT:	Black ostrich herl
BODY:	Black floss
RIBBING:	Oval gold tinsel
HACKLE:	Deep-orange-dyed hackle
THROAT:	Speckled guinea fowl dyed blue
WING:	Orange polar bear hair, over which is a bunch of natural brown bucktail, topped with a small bunch of yellow bucktail
SIDES:	Jungle cock
HEAD:	Black tying thread

◄ Hair wing patterns: (top row) Orange Blossom, Blue Vulture; (second row) Green Highlander, Rogers Fancy; (third row) Black Rat, Green Butt; (bottom row) Labrador, Cosseboom.

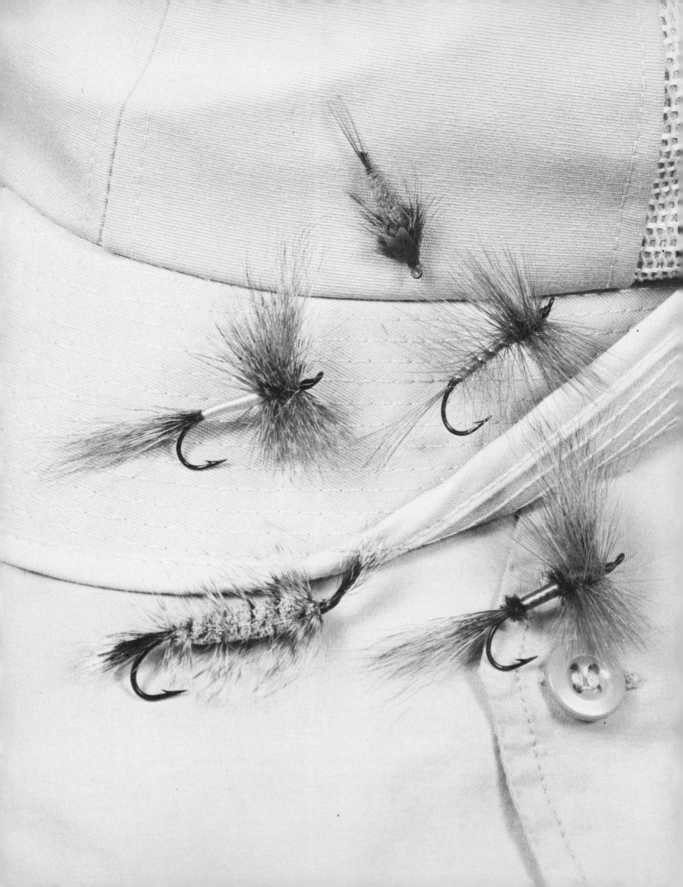

7

Dry Flies and Nymphs

It may be somewhat of a relief for anglers to note that one need not have any knowledge of entomology to successfully fish for the king of fishes with dry flies and nymphs. All one needs is a supply of flies in various colors and shapes and, of course, a good amount of courage.

The best-known dry flies used for salmon are the Wulff patterns developed by Lee Wulff, but one can actually use almost any of the more substantial trout flies for the purpose if they are dressed on the light-wire salmon hooks designed for just such artificials.

Fishing for salmon with dry flies and nymphs is not too well known outside North America, where it originated back in the early twenties and where it is still considered the ultimate in sport fishing. Some day perhaps, when everyone discovers the satisfaction of taking salmon on dry flies, other means will be ruled obsolete.

DRY FLIES

Dressing the Royal Wulff

THREAD:	Black, prewaxed 6/0
TAIL:	White calf or natural brown bucktail
BODY:	Two peacock herl butts, one at the tail, one at the back of the wing, separated by a center band of red floss
WING:	White calf or natural brown bucktail
HACKLE:	Three or four reddish-brown saddle hackles
HEAD:	Black tying thread

1. Tie in a bunch of hair on a light-wire salmon hook so it sits in the middle of the front half of the hook shank, with the tips projecting forward over the eye. If you use calf tail hair, some of the crinkles can be taken out by rolling the hair between the palms of your hands. Secure the hair tightly on top of the shank; the wing should be as long as the hook length.

2.–3. Pull all the hair up at a right angle and take several turns of thread directly up against the front of the hair. Now divide the hair bunch into two wings. Take a turn of thread around the base of the first bunch of hair in front of the tie-in point. Set this bunch upright, separate from the other bunch, then wind the tying thread around the hook shank to hold it there. Now do likewise with the other bunch of hair. Crisscross the tying thread between the two wings a couple of times. When the wing is set upright and divided as seen in the two photographs, you can apply a little cement on the windings. Trim the butt ends on a slant as shown.

4. Tie in a bunch of hair for the tail that is as long as the wing. Trim the butt ends on a slant so that they blend with those from the wing, and cover them with tying thread. This method gives you a nice, even underbody on which you can apply the body without any ugly bumps.

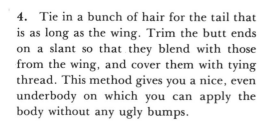

5.   Now tie in two peacock herls and wind the rear butt. Tie off the herl and lay the remainder alongside the underbody; then wind the tying thread over it to the middle of the shank. Tie in a length of red floss and wind it first to the rear up against the butt, then forward over the first layer to the middle, where it is tied off. Trim the surplus floss and wind the second herl butt in front of the floss segment. Tie off the peacock herl and trim away the surplus ends. Now wind the tying thread to midway between the peacock herl butt and the wing, where the hackle will be tied in.

6.   Tie in the hackles under the shank in the middle of the portion between the forward herl butt and the wing. Secure the butt ends of the stems along the underside and let the tying thread hang in front at a position midway between the wing and the hook eye.

7. To successfully wind this much hackle and still get it to sit in the proper manner often causes some trouble until you get the hang of it. It can be done. Grasp the first hackle and take a complete turn around the shank where it is tied in. The next turn should be tight against the rear of the wing, and the following turn as tight against the front of the wing as you can get it. Continue by winding the hackle forward a few more turns and tie it off. Trim the surplus and follow with the other hackles, winding them through the preceding ones, working the pliers with a back-and-forth motion so as not to bind down the fibers already in place. When all the hackle is on the hook hold the fibers out of the way with your fingers while winding a small head in front. Apply a few drops of clear head cement on the windings, and the fly is finished.

Note the proportions of the fly in the photograph: The rear herl butt is located above the hook point and the front butt approximately in the middle of the shank. This leaves the front half of the hook shank open except for the wing, which is located in the middle. Any less room at the front will make it difficult to accommodate the heavy amount of hackle that is often needed on this type of salmon dry fly, particularly on the Wulff patterns, which are often dressed as large as size 2.

Dressing the Bomber

The Bomber was first introduced to me some years ago by Ben Schley, when we were both at a Trout Unlimited meeting in Washington, D.C. Ben is, aside from being a superb writer and conservationist, also an avid salmon angler who nearly always has some sort of fly in his pocket, and if not, he is perfectly willing to make a drawing of the latest "killer." The fly's simplicity stuck in my mind, although I silently hoped I never would have to insult a salmon with such a "bomb" as long as I had fancy feathers in my box. I have since changed my mind. This fly may not look like a salmon fly, and certainly not like a Wulff, but it works better than most when salmon are taking.

HOOK:	Salmon dry fly hook sizes 2 to 8 (Or size 2 low-water)
THREAD:	Black, prewaxed 6/0 and tan size B nylon
TAIL:	Fairly heavy bunch of hair from the tail of an eastern pine squirrel or woodchuck guardhairs
WING:	A bunch of hair, same as for the tail, tied in close to and projecting forward over the eye in an upward direction
BODY:	Natural deer body hair spun and trimmed cigar shaped
HACKLE:	Grizzly, palmered

1. Attach the 6/0 prewaxed thread and tie in the tail and wing as shown. I now tie in an eighteen-inch length of heavy B thread in front like I would a ribbing and wind the fine thread to the rear, binding the B thread down along the hook shank in the process. When I get to the tail, I tie off and cut the thin thread. At that spot I make two half hitches with the B thread and let it hang where the first bunch of hair is to be applied. This procedure may seem strange to those who are deer hair specialists, but the thin thread will allow you to tie in the tail and wing hair more securely than will the heavy stuff.

2. Cut a bunch of deer body hair and spin it on the hook with your B thread at the tail position. When it is well distributed around the shank, wind the thread through the hair to the front of it and make a half hitch. Press the hair back slightly—it can still be done even though it is not spun on a bare shank. Apply a little cement on the half hitch and hair butts. You are ready now to apply the next hair bunch.

3. Continue to spin bunches of hair on the shank in the manner described in step 2. When the last bunch is applied, whip-finish the B thread and cut it.

4. Trim the deer body hair to a cigar-shaped style with your scissors. Attach the 6/0 thread at the tail position and tie in the hackle by the tip. Put a drop of cement on the windings. Now spiral the tying thread through the trimmed hair to the front and let it hang by the bobbin.

5. Palmer the hackle forward through the deer hair to the front and take a couple of extra turns before tying off and cutting the surplus. Finish off with a small head and apply some head cement.

The fly can also be dressed with white deer body hair, in which case the tail and wing are made with white calf tail. The hackle can be any color, like white, red, black, brown, etc. While I usually do not trim the hackle, it is often done by others.

SELECTED DRY FLY PATTERNS

Black Wulff

THREAD:	Black, prewaxed 6/0
TAIL:	Black moose or stiff black bear hair
BODY:	Pink floss wound over white silk and lacquered
WING:	Black moose or black bear hair
HACKLE:	Three or four furnace hackles
HEAD:	Black tying thread, lacquered

Cinnamon Sedge

THREAD:	Black, prewaxed 6/0
TAIL:	Ginger hackle fibers
BODY:	Ginger hackle tied palmer over yellow-green floss
WING:	Brown mottled turkey, fox squirrel, or woodchuck tied downwing
HACKLE:	Three or four ginger hackles wound after wing is attached
HEAD:	Black tying thread

Colonel Monell

THREAD:	Black, prewaxed 6/0
TAIL:	Grizzly hackle fibers
BODY:	Peacock herl
RIBBING:	Red floss
HACKLE:	Grizzly, palmered heavily
HEAD:	Black tying thread

Grey Wulff

THREAD:	Black, prewaxed 6/0
TAIL:	Natural brown bucktail
BODY:	Blue-gray wool or muskrat fur
WING:	Natural brown bucktail
HACKLE:	Gray blue dun hackle
HEAD:	Black tying thread

Grizzly Wulff

THREAD:	Black, prewaxed 6/0
TAIL:	Natural brown bucktail
BODY:	Pale yellow floss wound over white silk and lacquered
WING:	Natural brown bucktail
HACKLE:	Brown and grizzly, mixed
HEAD:	Black tying thread

The Grizzly Wulff

Mac Intosh

THREAD:	Black, prewaxed 6/0
WING:	Natural brown bucktail or fox squirrel tail fastened in the middle of hook, lying horizontally over the hook shank, and extending almost a hook length beyond hook bend
HACKLE:	Four brown saddle hackles wound heavy to front from middle of hook
HEAD:	Black tying thread

Pink Lady Palmer

THREAD:	Black, prewaxed 6/0
TAIL:	Light ginger hackle fibers, very stiff
BODY:	Pink floss ribbed with flat gold tinsel and palmered with ginger hackle
HACKLE:	Four very stiff light ginger saddle hackles fronted with two chartreuse yellow hackles
HEAD:	Black tying thread

Rat=Faced McDougal

THREAD:	Black, prewaxed 6/0
TAIL:	Stiff white bucktail hair
BODY:	Natural deer body hair, spun on the hook and trimmed to shape
WING:	White calf tail
HACKLE:	Three or four ginger saddle hackles
HEAD:	Black tying thread

The Soldier Palmer

Salmon Skater

HOOK:	A small light-wire salmon hook size 10 or 12
THREAD:	Black, prewaxed 6/0
HACKLE:	Four to six long-fibered stiff hackles wound and packed tightly on the shank from above the hook point to the eye, one and a half to two inches in diameter
HEAD:	Black tying thread; when thin lacquer is applied on the head, a small amount is also applied at the base of the front hackle and at the rear for durability

Soldier Palmer

THREAD:	Black, prewaxed 6/0
TAIL:	Dark ginger hackle fibers
BODY:	Red floss ribbed with oval gold tinsel and palmered with dark ginger saddle hackle
HACKLE:	Three or four dark ginger saddle hackles slightly longer in the fibers than the palmer hackle
HEAD:	Black tying thread

NYMPHS

Dressing the Salmon Fur Nymph

There are really no guide lines for the nymphs that work best for salmon. The ones I am most familiar with are simple, somber-colored artificials that are very similar to those used in trout fishing. Nymphs are the one area of salmon fly dressing where simplicity is in order, and where one can let imagination run unfettered by tradition. I believe the nymphs can be limited to light, medium, and dark shades dressed on low-water hooks.

THREAD:	Brown, prewaxed 6/0
TAIL:	Three fibers from a cock pheasant center tail
BODY:	Light brown, brown, or blackish brown Seal-Ex dubbing
RIBBING:	Medium oval gold tinsel wound counterclockwise
THORAX & LEGS:	Well-marked guardhair and fur from the back of a brown rabbit; natural for the light brown and brown nymph, but dyed blackish-brown for the darkest one
WINGCASE:	Trimmed latex strip, tinted
HEAD:	Butt end from latex wing

1. Tie in the three tail fibers securely on top of the shank above the hook point. The fibers should extend one and a half hook gaps beyond the bend. At the same spot, but underneath, tie in a length of gold tinsel and form a four-inch spinning loop with the tying thread. This is done by releasing eight inches of tying thread from the bobbin and doubling it over your index finger and back to the tie-in spot. Take three or four turns of thread around the shank and one directly around the loop tight against the shank before winging the thread forward to one-third body length from the eye.

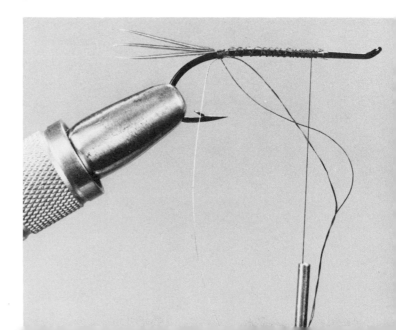

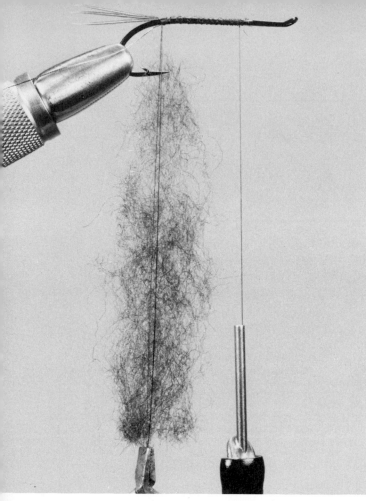

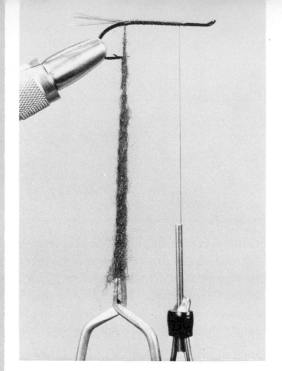

2. Insert a thin, tapered layer of Seal-Ex dubbing in the loop and clamp your heavy hackle pliers in the end. Now flip the pliers so they spin quickly, while aiding the dubbing around with your fingers to attain a tapered, rope-like dubbing piece.

3. Apply a little clear cement on the shank and wind on the dubbing, followed by the ribbing, which in this case is wound counterclockwise so it does not disappear in the dubbing. Leave one-third of the shank bare to accommodate the thorax, legs, and wingcase.

4. Cut a bunch of fur and guardhair from the edge of the rabbit skin with your scissors. Make sure the hair is long enough for the size nymph being dressed: about the length of the shank. Do not disturb the natural direction of the fibers.

Form a three-inch spinning loop directly in front of the completed body portion and insert the fur layer. Spread it out thinly so it occupies about one inch of space, then clamp your hackle pliers in the end of the loop close to the fur. Note that the longest portion—the guard hairs that become the legs—is to the left in the loop and reaches to the hook point, and a very small portion—the underfur, which becomes the thorax—is to the right. The smaller portion of fur can be trimmed to size either before it's inserted, or after it's spread out, to attain the right overall proportion.

5. Now flip the pliers so they spin rapidly to form the fur chenille shown in the photograph.

6. Moisten the fur chenille a little and massage it back with your fingers so it appears to be coming from one side of the loop, like a doubled hackle.

7. Wind the prepared fur chenille in front like you would a hackle collar, taking each turn directly in front of the previous one and stroking it back with a little moisture on your fingers in the process. Make sure to leave room in front for tying in the wing-case later.

8. Trim away the fur on top, as shown, to make a foundation for the wingcase, which is tied in next.

9. Cut a strip of heavy latex that is slightly wider than the body and trim out a notch in the end. The length of the latex should be about three-quarters inch (about 20 mm). Tie in the latex wingcase on top of the thorax portion, making sure the hook eye is still free in front. The wingcase reaches back about one-third of a bodylength.

10. Secure the wingcase tightly before making a whip finish and cutting the thread. Now trim away the surplus end of latex, leaving just a small portion to represent the head. Tint the latex with water-proof marking pen and wipe off the wing tips with a light marker for effect. Depending on the shade of the nymph, the tint should be chosen so the wingcase is always slightly darker than the rest of the nymph. Now you can apply a little cement on the thread windings underneath, taking care not to get any on the latex. This finishes the salmon fur nymph.

Prawns and Grubs

PRAWNS (Shrimp)

While it is generally believed that salmon flies do not represent anything in particular, there is one family of flies that were designed to imitate an important food source, namely the shrimp.

I recently acquired a *Hardy's Anglers Guide* dated 1937 which also served as their catalogue for that year. It contains some beautiful color plates, among which is one with natural baits and includes a small reddish-orange prawn. While these "naturals" should be effective for salmon, they are not suitable for casting with a fly rod. There are, however, some very fine imitations that have come along over the years. By far the best and most fascinating one is the General Practitioner, originated in England more than two decades ago by Colonel Esmond Drury, a distinguished English salmon angler who, as so many others, believed that salmon got their pinkish flesh color from feeding on shrimp (or prawns, as the English call them) during their long journeys in the ocean, and who apparently, like most dedicated salmon anglers, didn't want to mess with the natural shrimp.

Since salmon have undoubtedly become acquainted with the looks of shrimp during their long journeys in the ocean, there are times when prawn flies are extremely effective if they are properly dressed in an imitative fashion. Three of the best—the General Practitioner, the Shrimp fly, and the Icelandic Krabla fly—are subjects for the tying instructions in this chapter and will perhaps inspire the reader to use his own imagination to further develop some imitative shrimp.

Dressing the General Practitioner

HOOK:	Double low-water, sizes 2 to 6
THREAD:	Red, prewaxed 6/0
ANTENNAE:	15 to 20 bucktail fibers dyed hot orange
HEAD:	Small reddish orange neck feather from a golden pheasant (This feather sits high on the neck of the bird above the metallic-colored feathers)
BODY:	Hot orange wool, seal's fur, or Seal-Ex, fairly thin.
RIBBING:	Oval gold tinsel
HACKLE (legs):	Hackle dyed hot orange, palmered over the body
BACK:	Two reddish orange breast feathers from a golden pheasant, tied flat
EYES:	Golden pheasant tippet with center cut out to form a V shape, lacquered
HEAD:	Red tying thread

The original dressing, as it was introduced in England many years ago, had three breast feathers tied over the back, spaced out. The long hooks available then cannot be obtained today, and the length of the low-water hook leaves room for only two sections.

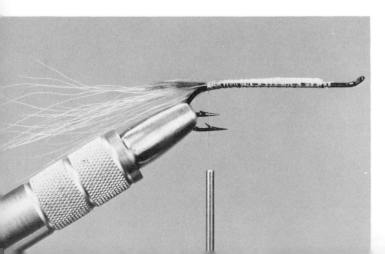

1. Tie in the Bucktail fibers at the bend directly above the barb of the hook. The tips should be pointing slightly down and extend a body length and a half beyond the bend. Now tie in the reddish orange neck feather with the good side up to represent the head. The fibers should be slightly bunched together over the bucktail and extend a hook-gap length beyond the bend. Bind down the material ends on the shank to serve as an underbody.

2. Select a hot orange neck hackle with the fibers at the butt end about a hook gap and a half long. Tie it in at the same spot as the other material, together with a six-inch length of hot orange wool and a length of oval gold tinsel, which is tied in under the shank.

3. Wind the wool to the middle of the hook shank to form the rear body half, then follow with three or four turns of ribbing spiraled over it. Do not cut the surplus tinsel, since it will be used to form the front body later. The hackle is now palmered forward, with each turn of hackle placed closely behind each turn of tinsel. Tie it off in front of the wool body and cut the surplus hackle.

4. The eyes are made from a golden pheasant tippet feather (left). The lower fibers have been pulled off and the center trimmed out to form a V shape. Apply a little cement on each leg to hold the fibers together. Prepare a golden pheasant breast feather like the one shown to the right in the photograph. Both the tippet and the breast feather should be long enough to reach a little beyond the bend of the hook, measured from the front of the finished body portion.

5. Trim away the hackle fibers on top of the rear body portion and tie in the golden pheasant breast feather. It should lie flat over the body with the tip projecting slightly past the hook bend. Directly over the breast feather, tie in the tippet so the legs project out at the same angle on both sides of the hook shank and reach only to a point above the bend.

6. Now tie in another hackle that is slightly shorter in the fibers than the first one. Wind the wool over the front half of the shank, followed by the ribbing, then palmer the hackle over the body and tie it off. Make sure that there is room in front for the last back feather and a small head.

7. Trim away the hackle fibers on top and tie in a second golden pheasant breast feather that has been prepared like the first one. It should reach from the tie-in spot in front to the middle of the tippet feather. Cut the surplus feather and wind a smooth head before applying several coats of head cement on the windings. This completes the General Practitioner.

Dressing the Shrimp Fly

HOOK:	Double, sizes 2 to 8
THREAD:	Black, prewaxed 6/0
TAG:	Fine oval silver tinsel
TAIL HACKLE:	Reddish-orange breast feather from a golden pheasant
BODY:	Rear half, yellow floss veiled top and bottom with Indian crow and butted with a white hackle collar; front half, black floss veiled with Indian crow like the rear
RIBBING:	Oval silver tinsel, rear ribbing slightly finer than the front
FRONT HACKLE:	Black rooster neck hackle, fairly stiff
HEAD:	Black tying thread

Indian Crow feathers are no longer available. I substitute small hen neck hackles that have been dyed reddish orange.

1. First form a tag that starts above the hook point and continues down the bend with five or six turns of tinsel. Directly in front of it, and by the tip, tie in a reddish orange body feather with fibers twice as long as the hook shank, and wind it as a hackle collar as previously explained in dressing the Rusty Rat hair-wing. When the feather is wound and tied off, tie in a three-inch length of fine oval silver fastening it under the shank, directly in front of the hackle. Now take the tying thread to the middle of the body and tie in a four-inch length of yellow floss.

2. Wind the yellow floss body, and then spiral the ribbing forward with three or four turns. Now tie on the two Indian crow feathers for veilings, top and bottom, lying flat. The tips of the feathers should reach just slightly beyond the bend of the hook. The white butt hackle is now tied and wound in as a hackle collar. The fibers should be just slightly shorter than the length of the Indian crow veiling.

3. Form the front body section. The tips of the Indian crow veilings should extend to the rear of the yellow floss body. Wind the black hackle collar in front in the usual manner—the fibers should be long enough to reach to the hook bend. Wind a small head, and the fly is finished.

Dressing the Krabla Fly

This unusual artificial was brought back to me from Iceland by my good friend Art Lee. It is the native Icelandic angler's theory that the long hackle-stem antennae dressed in the rear of the fly create a commotion that attracts the fish. The salmon is then enticed to strike the visible part of the fly, namely, the body and marabou tail.

HOOK: Double, sizes 2 to 8

THREAD: Red, prewaxed 6/0

ANTENNAE: Four stripped hackle stems, two pink and two white

TAIL: White marabou

BODY: Two large reddish-pink and one white neck or saddle hackle wound close on the shank and trimmed to shape

RIBBING: Oval silver tinsel

HEAD: Red tying thread

The Krabla fly can be dressed in two other colors as well. The Green Krabla has green antennae, tail, and body—with a yellow head. The Yellow and Black Krabla has yellow antennae and rear body half, black tail and front body half—with a yellow head.

1. Strip all the fibers off two pink and two white neck hackles. They should be three times as long as the hook measured from the eye to the bend. It is best to pick the hackles so they are not too much longer than that to start with to get them as tapered and fine at the end as possible. Tie them in at the hook bend, two on top of the shank and two directly underneath. Try to get them to curve out and away from each other.

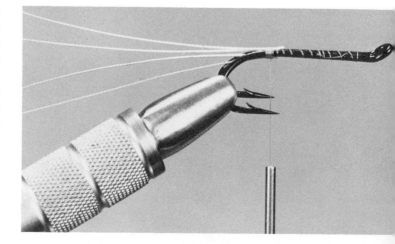

2. Now tie in the marabou for the tail, which should project about a body length beyond the bend. At the same spot, tie in a four-inch length of oval silver ribbing, fastened under the shank, together with the three body hackles, which are tied in on top. Wind the tying thread forward.

3. Wind the hackles forward on the shank with close turns. I find it best to double back the fibers when taking the first complete turn, as I like these fibers to slant back and blend a little with the tail when the body is trimmed later. Now spiral the ribbing forward through the hackle without winding down the fibers. Tie off the tinsel and cut the surplus. Hold the fibers out of the way and wind a small head, then tie off and cut the thread.

4. Trim the body so that it is cylindrical and tapered down in front as shown in the photograph. Note that some of the fibers from the first turn of hackle are not trimmed. This gives the fly a more compact look and adds life. If the trimming gives you trouble, hold it in the rear and trim it from the front with your scissors parallel to the body. To finish the Krabla, wind a small head and apply some head cement.

SELECTED GRUB PATTERNS

Artificial grub flies are relatively unknown to anglers in North America, at least for salmon fishing. However, they do bear some resemblance to the popular woolly worms used for trout fishing, and one could easily be led to believe that the grubs represent the large caterpillars and other such insects that often exist near the river during summer and early fall.

By using the tying instructions for the various parts already given throughout the book and studying the photographs of the flies, it is hardly necessary to repeat them for these simple dressings. I shall, therefore, merely give the material list for the two grubs that seem the most fascinating and leave the rest to the reader.

Jungle Hornet

HOOK:	Single or double, sizes 2/0 to 6
THREAD:	Black, prewaxed
TAG:	Fine oval silver tinsel
TAIL:	Small golden pheasant breast feather *reddish orange* with a jungle cock nail on each side, half as long as the feather
BODY:	Alternate bands of yellow and black wool or chenille in two sections, starting rearmost with yellow
JUNGLE COCK:	One pair, the middle slightly larger than those at the tail, tied in before the hackle is wound; increase the size slightly of the pair in front.
HACKLE:	Furnace hackle feathers tied in three separate positions, one at the tail, one in the middle in front of the rear body half, and one at the head, all tied in as collars; increase the size of each hackle, the smallest at the rear, the middle slightly larger, and the front the largest
HEAD:	Black tying thread

Due to the restrictions on jungle cock, these feathers may be left out. The fly will still be both effective and attractive.

HORNET   The Tippet Grub

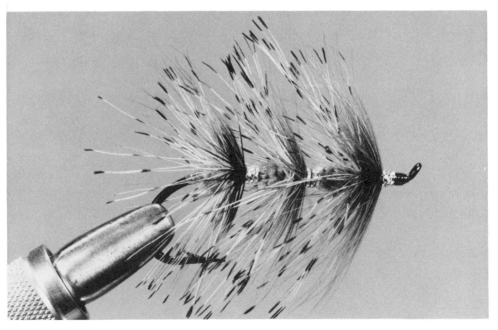

The Jungle Hornet

Grub

Tippet Grub

HOOK: Single or double, sizes 2/0 to 6

THREAD: Black, prewaxed 6/0

TAG: Gold tinsel and scarlet seal's fur or wool

BODY: In two equal halves, each beginning with three turns of round silver tinsel matching the fly size, followed by green wool butted in the middle by a tippet and hackle collar slightly longer than those for the butt

HACKLE: Same as butt and middle hackles, but slightly larger

HEAD: Oval silver tinsel and black tying thread

EM-TE 31058 Vessigebro
Art. nr T-757 Storl. 2
Färg

9

Flies on Waddington Shanks and Treble Hooks

The Waddington shank, with an articulating treble hook permanently attached in the posterior end, and the Esmond Drury long-shank treble hook can at best be described as unusual, perhaps even unnecessary in view of the fact that treble hooks are illegal on some North American rivers. But they are nevertheless fascinating and extremely popular elsewhere in the world for their hooking qualities. My Danish friend Preben Torp Jacobsen sent me some samples of the Waddington shank and the Drury treble hooks with a message from Magrete Thomsen in Vassegebro, Sweden, telling me how popular they are and urging me to include them in this book. I hope it will benefit those who still have access to rivers where treble hooks are legal.

FLIES ON WADDINGTON SHANKS

The Waddington shank is similar to those of regular salmon hooks in both size and appearance. However, instead of the normal bend, it has another eye at the posterior end by which the treble hook of a suitable size is attached. To prevent the hook from just sitting loose and risking entanglement with the body, there should be a piece of nylon connected between the shaft and the treble hook. This is tied in before the fly is dressed, as explained in the tying instructions that follow. Like the tube flies, almost any of the orthodox salmon flies—even the Muddler Minnow—can be dressed on the Waddington shank if one uses a little imagination. The Thunder and Lightning, Jock Scott, and Lady Caroline are typical patterns that are suitable for the Waddington shank. By following the tying instructions and making reference to other chapters, they can be fairly simple.

Dressing the Waddington Thunder and Lightning

HOOK:	See "Waddington Shanks" and "Treble Hooks" in chapter 1 and step 1 in the tying instructions.
THREAD:	Black, prewaxed 6/0
TAG:	Fine oval gold tinsel and yellow floss dressed on the treble hook
BUTT:	Black ostrich herl dressed on the treble hook
BODY:	Black silk or rayon floss
RIBBING:	Flat gold tinsel and twist (round tinsel)
HACKLE:	Bright orange palmered over floss body from the first turn of tinsel
WING:	A black heron hackle wound as a collar with fibers extending back to the bend of the treble hook
THROAT:	Blue-dyed guinea fowl body feather wound as a collar
HEAD:	Black tying thread

In some countries, including the United States, the heron hackle is not available, and you should use one of the substitutes mentioned in chapter 1. A second alternative that works especially well on this type of fly is the soft hair that comes from the tip of a natural black squirrel tail. This is tied in sparingly instead of the heron as a collar.

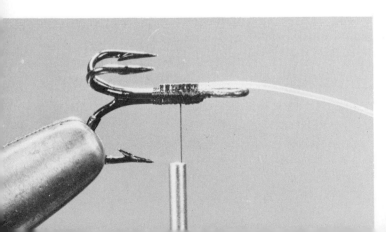

1. A size 8 treble hook will be about right for the size 2/0 shaft I have chosen for this fly. Place the hook in the vise and attach a two-inch length of nylon leader about fifteen pounds test. Secure it tightly with tying thread in such a manner that it does not extend farther back than to the middle of the shank.

2. Tie in the tag and butt as previously explained in chapter 3. Now draw the long nylon end through the eye, and you are ready to attach the hook to the shaft.

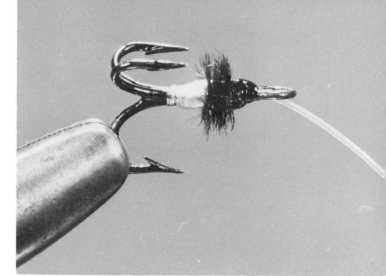

3. Attach the treble hook in the eye of the shank and close it tightly with a pair of pliers.

4. Secure the shank in the vise by the posterior eye and attach the tying thread. Tie down the nylon along the shank, and make sure that it is pulled tight enough to keep the treble hook sitting by itself parallel to the shank. Trim the nylon so that it is a quarter inch short of the front eye.

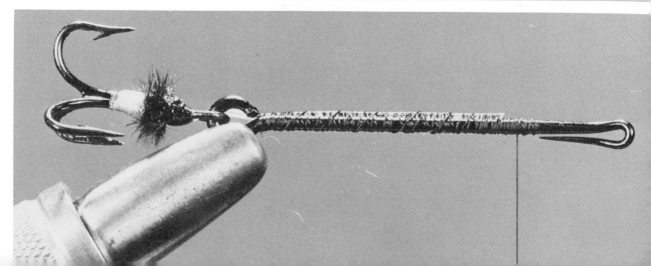

5. Now dress the body according to the pattern you have chosen; this is Thunder and Lightning. The twist (round tinsel) should follow directly behind the flat tinsel, and the palmer body hackle tightly behind it. When the body is finished, tie in a heron hackle in front, by the butt. The fibers on that hackle should be long enough to reach the bend of the treble hook when wound.

6. Double the heron hackle and wind it as a collar in front. Use as much hackle as needed to make a good and fairly dense appearance. Now strip one side of the blue-dyed guinea and wind it in front of the heron hackle. Two or three turns will suffice. The fibers should reach down about a third of a wing length. Wind a small head, and the fly is finished.

SELECTED DRESSINGS ON WADDINGTON SHANKS

Jorgensen's Waddington Muddler

THREAD:	Black, prewaxed 6/0
TAIL:	Short grizzly hackle fibers dyed brown and tied on the treble hook
BODY:	Golden yellow floss
RIBBING:	Oval gold tinsel
HACKLE:	A soft grizzly hackle dyed brown, palmered over the body from first turn of ribbing. Front fibers should reach back to middle of body when wound.
WING:	Gray squirrel tail hair set sparsely as a collar and extending to bend of treble hook
COLLAR:	Well-marked dark deer body hair reaching to middle of body
HEAD:	Spun deer body hair, trimmed

The head on this Muddler is formed by the butt ends of the hair collar, without any additional deer body hair applied. This is done by leaving the butt ends quite long and tied in closer to the eye than normal. When the butt ends are well flared out, I wind the tying thread through the fibers and to the front, pulling each turn tight. When the tying thread reaches the front of the hair, close to the eye, I brush back the hair with my fingers and hold it while winding a small head. Then I trim the deer body hair to the Muddler shape from behind only. This method makes a less dense head that is more like it was intended by Don Gapen, who designed the Muddler Minnow many years ago.

Jorgensen's Waddington Jock Scott

THREAD:	Black, prewaxed 6/0
TAG:	Fine oval silver tinsel and yellow floss tied on the treble hook

BUTT: Black ostrich herl tied on the treble hook

BODY: Rear half, yellow floss; front half, black floss

RIBBING: Oval silver tinsel

HACKLE: Soft black hackle palmered over black floss only; longest fibers should reach to middle of body when wound.

WING: A few yellow, red, and blue-dyed polar bear hairs mixed and set as a collar with the tips reaching to the herl butt, outside of which are a few gray squirrel tail hairs and a gray mallard flank feather dyed brown, both dressed as a collar and extending to bend of treble hook

THROAT: Speckled guinea fowl body feather wound as a collar and extending down one-third of a wing length

HEAD: Black tying thread

Jorgensen's Waddington Lady Caroline

THREAD: Black, prewaxed 6/0

BODY: One olive green and two light brown strands of wool wound together side by side. Body should be fairly thin.

RIBBING: Oval gold tinsel

HACKLE: Soft blue dun gray hackle, palmered from the first turn of the tinsel. Longest fibers should reach to the middle of the body when wound.

WING: A few gray-dyed polar bear hairs set as a collar and extending to the bend of the treble hook, outside of which is a gray mallard flank feather dyed brown and wound as a collar, with the tips reaching to the end of the posterior eye of the shank

THROAT: A small golden pheasant breast feather wound as a collar and extending down one-third on dyed brown mallard wing

HEAD: Black tying thread

SELECTED DRESSINGS ON ESMOND DRURY'S TREBLE HOOKS

Esmond Drury's treble hook salmon flies are dressed in the same manner as any other salmon fly. More specific instructions would merely be a repetition of previous chapters. Feather-wing patterns can be converted to hair-wings on Drury hooks, for example, by tying the appropriate color hair completely around the shank in a mixed bunch.

Actually, the flies have no wings as such, other than hair and feathers attached in front as a collar extending just a hook gap beyond the bends of the three hooks. When hackle feathers are called for in the body they should always be doubled and wound whole, without stripping one side. They sit much better and much fuller in that fashion.

I am including three dressings that I have found particularly interesting, but one can, of course, convert any pattern to this hook, including the Shrimp and Krabla flies described in another chapter.

Silver Doctor

(Color Scheme by the Author)

HOOK:	Long shank treble hook, any size
THREAD:	Black, prewaxed 6/0
TAG:	Fine oval silver tinsel and golden yellow floss
BUTT:	Red wool or Seal-Ex
BODY:	Flat silver tinsel
RIBBING:	Oval silver tinsel
WING:	A few yellow, red, and blue-dyed polar bear hairs mixed and set as a collar, over which is a teal flank feather wound as a collar; both materials extending a hook gap beyond the bend
HACKLE:	A blue-dyed hackle wound as a collar with tips reaching to the hook point
HEAD:	Red tying thread

The Silver Doctor, Drury treble hook

Port and Starboard

HOOK:	Long shank treble hook, any size
THREAD:	Black, prewaxed 6/0
TAIL:	Golden pheasant tippet fibers, fairly short
TAG:	Fine oval gold tinsel
BODY:	Rear half, red floss; front half, medium green floss
RIBBING:	Oval gold tinsel
WING:	Soft black hair, set as a collar
HEAD:	Black tying thread

The above is described from a fly sent to me by the distinguished Danish fly dresser, Preben Torp Jacobsen.

Orange Blossom

HOOK:	Long shank treble hook, any size
THREAD:	Black, prewaxed 6/0
TAG:	Fine oval silver tinsel and yellow floss
BUTT:	Black ostrich herl
BODY:	Flat embossed silver tinsel
WING:	Natural pale brown bucktail set sparsely as a collar
HACKLE:	Bright orange hackle wound as a collar, extending to the hook point
HEAD:	Black tying thread

C
Pentland Firth
Dunnet Hd
Duncansby Hd
John O'Groats
Thurso
C. Wrath L.H.
L. Eriboll
Durness
Tongue
Butt of Lewis L.H.
Halladale
L. Loyal
CAITHNESS
Wick
Ben Hope 3040 ft
Eddrachillis Bay
Unapool
Kinbrace
Lybster
Stornoway
Broad B.
SUTHERLAND
Lochinver
Ben Klibreck 3154 ft
Enard Bay
3273 ft
Ben More Assynt
Loch Shin
North Minch
Helmsdale
Lairg
Brora
L. Broom
Greenstone Pt
Ullapool
Oykell
Dornoch
Dornoch Firth
Tarbert
Shiant Is
Ben Dearg 3547 ft
Tarbat Ness L.H.
L. Ewe
Tain
Moray Firth
Rubna Hunish
ROSS & CROMARTY
Lossiemouth
Gairloch
Alness
Ben Wyvis 3429 ft
Cromarty
Elgin
L. Snizort
L. Maree
Fannich
Fortrose
Buckie
L. Torridon
Nairn
Forres
Keith
Deveron
MORAY
NAIRN
Portree
Inverness
Dufftown
Huntly
BANFF
Spey
Grantown on Spey
Findhorn
L. Ness
Alford
Isle of Skye
Cuillin Hills
Broadford
INVERNESS
Aviemore
Don
ABERDE
Cairngorms
Monadhliath Mts
Kingussie
Ben Macdhui
Ballater
4296 ft
Dee
SCOTLAND
Rhum
Mallaig
L. Lochy
L. Laggan
Eigg
Arisaig
Morar
Caledonian Canal
Nr. Esk
Muck
4406 ft
ANGUS
Fort William
Ben Nevis
Brechin
L. Shiel
Salen
Pitlochry
Kirriemuir
Coll
Tobermory
L. Sunart
Ballachulish
Blairgowrie
Forfar
Morven
L. Linnhe
Dunkeld
Sidlaw Hills
L. Etive
Bridge of Orchy
Dundee
Staffa
Connel Ferry
Mull
Oban
L. Earn
Comrie
Perth
Tay
Crianlarich
Crieff
Cupar
Iona
L. Awe
GRAMPIAN
Katrine
Callander
Ochil Hills
Kinross
L. Leven
FIFE
Firth of Lorne
Inveraray
Arrochar
Aberfoyle
CL.
K.
ARGYLL
Forth
Alloa
Cowdenbeath
Methil
L. Fyne
Cowal
L. Long
L. Lomond
Stirling
Kirkcaldy
Inchkeith
Colonsay
DUN.
STIRLING
Dunfermline
Jura
Helensburgh
Leith
Sd. of Jura
Ardrishaig
Dumbarton
Falkirk
Greenock
Clyde
Glasgow
W.L.
Edinburgh
Tarbert
Coatbridge
MIDLOTHIAN
Paisley
Port Askaig
Rothesay
Motherwell
Largs
RENFREW
Pentland Hills
Moorfoot Hills
Islay
Bute
Hamilton
Gigha
Lanark
Carstairs
Peebles
Ardrossan
Kilmarnock
LANARK
L. Indaal
I. of
Port Ellen
PEEBLES

10

Dee Strip-Wings and Spey Flies

Dee strip-wing and Spey fly patterns hail from Scotland and are characteristically different in appearance from the beautifully garnished Jock Scotts and Silver Grays. Their usefulness, however, is very much in evidence judging from their popularity around the world. The slim, sparsely dressed bodies and wings make them perfectly suited for fishing the fast, cold rivers of the early season when flies must sink deeper than normal and do so fairly quickly.

The hooks on which both patterns should be dressed are called "Dee" salmon hooks after the River Dee. They are similar to the regular English salmon hook in shape and wire diameter, but the shank is a little longer and very similar to a low-water hook. Unfortunately, the Dee hooks are no longer available on a regular basis and are not obtainable at all in the United States. Instead one can dress the flies on English low-water hooks, or better yet, on a regular Mustad #36890. The latter, incidentally, is 1X longer than the regular English salmon hook. This means that a size 2 Mustad has the same shank length and wire diameter as a size 1 regular English hook, which makes the Mustad come very close to the elusive Dee.

In general, dressing the Dee strip-wing and Spey flies is not different from what has previously been described in other preceding chapters, with the notable exception of the wing style and some added techniques for dressing the bodies.

DEE STRIP-WINGS

Dressing the Akroyd

(White Winged)

THREAD:	Black, prewaxed 6/0
TAG:	Flat silver tinsel
TAIL:	Golden pheasant crest and tippet in strands
BODY:	Rear half, light orange seal's fur or Seal-Ex; front half, black floss
RIBBING:	Oval silver tinsel over rear body half, flat silver tinsel and twist over front half
HACKLE:	Lemon-dyed hackle over the orange seal's fur, black heron hackle over the black floss
THROAT:	Teal flank feather, wound as a collar and tied under
WING:	Two strips of white goose shoulder feather set flat and divided
CHEEKS:	Jungle cock, slanting downward
HEAD:	Black tying thread

The Akroyd can also be dressed with strips from a cinnamon turkey tail, or as a hair wing, which is very popular on some Canadian rivers. The body is the same, but the wing is made from natural brown or white bucktail for dressing the larger flies, and the same color but softer hair, like calf tail, for the smaller flies.

1. Dress the Akroyd body as shown in the photograph, using the instructions given previously in the chapters dealing with simple strip wings and fully dressed flies. When the heron hackle has been tied in by the tip and palmered forward over the black floss, take a couple of extra turns close together in front. The longest fibers should then extend back to just slightly beyond the hook bend.

Prepare the throat by stripping one side of a teal flank feather and winding it in front of the heron; the tips of the teal should reach almost to the hook point. Measure it and tie it under the hook as a throat. On smaller flies (4 to 10) I often use large, soft blue dun neck hackle instead of heron and tie in the teal as a false hackle. The jungle cock cheeks, which are half a body length, are now tied in on each side at a downward slant, pointing directly at the hook point.

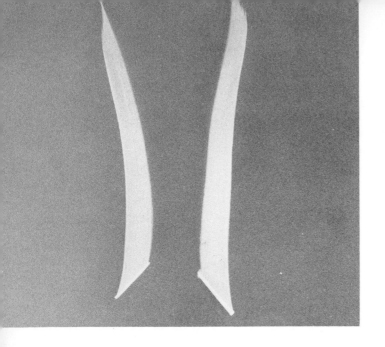

2. Prepare the two wing strips as shown. In this case the right strip (to the right in the photograph) is used for the right wing, and the left strip for the left wing. If possible, it is best to leave a little stem at the butt ends so that the feather will not collapse when drawn into place after being tied in. The strips should be long enough for the tips to project just slightly beyond the hook bend, and with a good portion extending forward in front as a "handle" for drawing them into place. The width depends on the size fly being dressed, but is usually about one-third hook gap.

3. Hold the tying thread at a right angle above the hook shank. Place the right wing strip flat against the side of the body at a downward angle and hold it with your thumb. In front, the tying thread is on the outside of the feather strip, and the lower wing edge (when tied in it becomes the outer wing edge) crosses the top side of the shank at the tie-in spot, where it will sit when the wing is fastened later. In the rear, the tip of the slanted down wing strip should extend to just slightly beyond the hook bend.

4. While still holding the strip in the position described in step 3, fasten it not-too-tightly on the shank with three or four turns of thread. In doing so, the base of the strip will roll over the shank on top at the tie-in spot as it should. Now grasp the wing strip and the butt end handle with your fingers and draw the rolled-over fibers toward you so all the tied-down fibers occupy only the nearest half of the hook shank, as shown in this top view. The wing strip should sit flatly and horizontally at an outward angle. (See side view of finished fly in step 7.)

5. Now reverse the tying thread and attach the left wing in the same manner. Make sure the fibers are lying alongside those of the right wing on top of the shank.

6. Close-up of correct position of the wing strips in relation to each other when tied in.

7. Trim away the butt ends and reverse the tying thread back before finishing the small head.

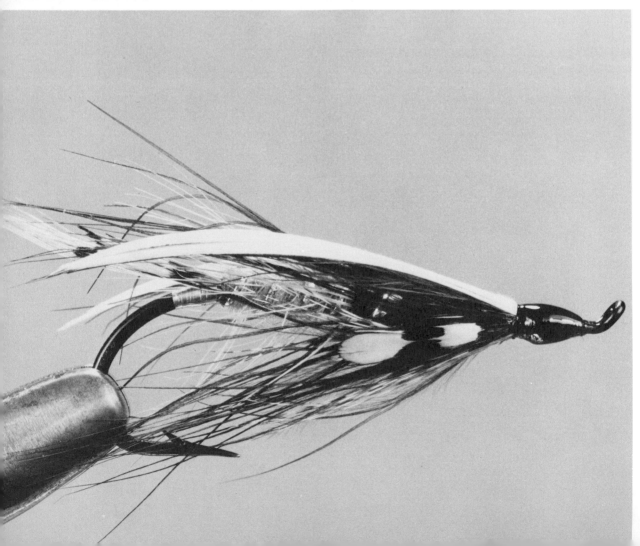

SPEY FLIES

Dressing the Gray Heron

THREAD:	Black, prewaxed 6/0
BODY:	Rear third, lemon-colored wool; front two-thirds, black wool; both dressed slim
RIBBING:	Flat silver tinsel, oval gold tinsel, and fine silver tinsel
HACKLE:	Gray heron hackle
THROAT:	Speckled guinea fowl body feather
WING:	Two brown mallard strips, set low
HEAD:	Black tying thread

The body of a Spey fly is not more difficult to dress than any other salmon fly body, though it looks different. The body materials on these flies should be applied very sparsely to produce a slim look. While the hackle in this case is heron, the spey hackle, for which the fly is known, is used on other similar flies. These metallic black, brown, or plain gray feathers sit on the side of the tails on some roosters. (See chapter 1.) When using a spey hackle, it is necessary to strip off the fibers on one side, or it will be too heavy and dense.

Unlike almost all the other styles of salmon flies, the dominant feature of the Spey series is the hackle, especially since the winging is usually a somber tone, and the spey fly presents a most unusual profile.

The heron hackle is tied on by the butt in the rear of the body, then doubled and spiralled forward in a clockwise direction with each turn placed midway between each turn of gold tinsel. The longest fibers of the hackle should be the same as one full body length.

The fine silver tinsel that was tied in with the ribbing is then wound counterclockwise to the front, binding down the stem of the heron hackle after it has been wound in. Be careful not to bind down any of the hackle fibers, which can be manipulated out of the way with a dubbing needle: it is these free-flowing fibers which give the fly its fish appeal. Nonetheless, I sometimes find this to be a troublesome process, and so instead draw the hackle stem up close behind the gold tinsel as it is wound to protect it from being torn by the fish's teeth, leaving the silver tinsel out altogether.

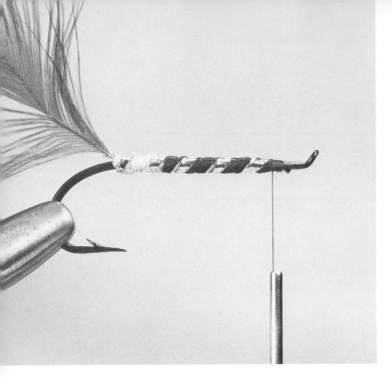

1. This is how the body materials should appear under the hackle, which is doubled and spiralled forward in a clockwise motion so that it actually appears as in step 2.

2. The guinea fowl feather for the throat is now stripped off of one side, tied in by the tip, and wound as a collar. The fibers should reach almost to the hook point. For this fly, I don't tie all the fibers under as a throat as is customary. I leave a few on top, so that they, together with the few extra turns of heron, can form a small foundation or underwing for the fragile mallard strips.

3. Cut two brown mallard strips, fairly wide, and with the same general curvature. It is best to leave a piece of stem in the butt ends so they will not come apart. These are cut from two feathers that are taken from opposite sides of the bird. One of the characteristics of Spey fly wings is their coloration. The tip portions are generally brown, and the roots closer to the tie-in spot are gray. The pronounced curvature of these strips makes them well suited for Spey fly wings, which lie very low over the body.

The strip to the right in the photograph is for the right wing, and the other is for the left (far) wing.

4. Tie in the wings as explained in chapter 3 ("Preparing and Tying in the Wing"). As the feathers in this case are usually curved by nature, humping is not necessary, unless of course you have picked some feathers that are uncommonly straight. Aside from the characteristics mentioned in step 2, the Spey fly wings must sit very low over the body and form a rooflike structure where the upper wing edges meet exactly above the middle of the hook shank. The tips must reach no farther back than the hook bend. When the wings are set, the surplus ends are trimmed away, and a very small head is wound in front.

SELECTED DEE STRIP DRESSINGS

Akroyd

See tying instructions.

Balmoral

THREAD:	Black, prewaxed 6/0
TAG:	Fine round or oval silver tinsel
TAIL:	Golden pheasant crest and tippet in strands
BUTT:	Black ostrich herl
BODY:	Rear half, green seal's fur; front half, dark blue seal's fur (substitute Seal-Ex)
RIBBING:	Flat silver tinsel and silver lace
HACKLE:	Black heron
THROAT:	Widgeon (or substitute mallard or teal)
WING:	Two strips of cinnamon turkey tail
CHEEKS:	Jungle cock, slanting downward
HEAD:	Black tying thread

Black Eagle

THREAD:	Black, prewaxed 6/0
TAG:	Flat silver tinsel
TAIL:	Golden pheasant crest and Indian crow
BODY:	Black seal's fur or Seal-Ex
RIBBING:	Flat and oval silver tinsel
HACKLE:	Black-dyed marabou (substitute for eagle feather) with one side stripped, wound from third turn of tinsel

WING:	Two strips of white-tipped turkey tail, dark
HEAD:	Black tying thread

Dunt

THREAD:	Black, prewaxed 6/0
TAG:	Silver wire and pale blue floss
TAIL:	Golden pheasant crest and two jungle cock feathers set back to back
BODY:	Equal sections of yellow, orange, and fiery brown seal's fur or Seal-Ex substitute, dressed thin and picked out tapered
RIBBING:	Flat silver tinsel and twist (round tinsel)
THROAT:	Teal flank feather
WING:	Two strips of black-barred, white-tipped turkey tail set like in Akroyd
CHEEKS:	Jungle cock feathers slanting downward
HEAD:	Black tying thread

Glentana

THREAD:	Black, prewaxed 6/0
TAG:	Fine oval silver tinsel and lemon floss
TAIL:	Golden pheasant crest and strands of red breast feather
BODY:	Rear third, orange seal's fur; remainder, claret seal's fur; body dressed thin and well picked out
RIBBING:	Flat silver tinsel and twist (round tinsel)
HACKLE:	Black heron hackle from third turn of tinsel
THROAT:	Widgeon (or substitute mallard or teal)
WING:	Two strips of cinnamon turkey tail, set like on Akroyd
HEAD:	Black tying thread

Jock O'Dee

THREAD:	Black, prewaxed 6/0
TAG:	Fine round silver tinsel
TAIL:	Golden pheasant crest and Indian crow
BODY:	Rear two-fifths, lemon floss; remainder, black floss
RIBBING:	Flat silver tinsel and twist (round tinsel)
HACKLE:	Gray heron from third turn of tinsel
THROAT:	Widgeon (substitute mallard or teal)
WING:	Two strips of cinnamon turkey tails set like on Akroyd
HEAD:	Black tying thread

Moonlight

THREAD:	Black, prewaxed 6/0
TAG:	Flat silver tinsel
TAIL:	Golden pheasant crest and two jungle cock feathers set back to back
BODY:	Rear half, silver tinsel veiled above and below with blue chatterer (or substitute) back to back; front half, black floss
RIBBING:	Fine oval silver tinsel over flat tinsel, wider oval gold tinsel over black floss
HACKLE:	Black heron over black floss only
THROAT:	Speckled guinea fowl body feather
WING:	Two strips of cinnamon turkey tail set like on Akroyd
HEAD:	Black tying thread

Yellow Eagle

THREAD:	Black, prewaxed 6/0
TAG:	Flat silver tinsel

TAIL:	Golden pheasant crest and strands of red breast feather
BODY:	Lemon, bright orange, scarlet, and fiery brown seal's fur (or Seal-Ex) in equal sections; should be well picked out
RIBBING:	Wide flat silver tinsel and twist (round tinsel)
HACKLE:	Yellow-dyed marabou feather with one side stripped (substitute for eagle hackle)
THROAT:	Widgeon (or substitute mallard or teal)
WING:	Two strips of light-mottled gray turkey tail set as on Akroyd
HEAD:	Black tying thread

SELECTED SPEY FLY DRESSINGS

Black Heron

THREAD:	Black, prewaxed 6/0
TAG:	Flat silver tinsel
TAIL:	Golden pheasant crest, short
BODY:	Two turns of yellow floss; remainder, black floss; dressed very thin
RIBBING:	Oval silver tinsel
HACKLE:	Black heron from third turn of tinsel
THROAT:	A few turns of speckled guinea fowl body feather with tips reaching to hook point
WING:	Two dark gray goose quill strips
HEAD:	Black tying thread

Gray Heron

See tying instructions.

Brown Heron

THREAD:	Red, prewaxed 6/0
BODY:	Rear two-thirds, orange floss; remainder, hot orange seal's fur (or Seal-Ex)
RIBBING:	Flat and oval silver tinsel
HACKLE:	Gray heron wound from second turn of tinsel
THROAT:	Teal flank feather
WING:	Two strips of brown mallard
HEAD:	Red tying thread

Carron

THREAD:	Black, prewaxed 6/0
BODY:	Orange wool
RIBBING:	Flat silver tinsel, scarlet floss, and silver wire
HACKLE:	Black heron wound from fourth turn of tinsel
THROAT:	Teal flank feather
WING:	Two brown mallard strips
HEAD:	Black tying thread

Gold Riach

THREAD:	Black, prewaxed 6/0
BODY:	Rear one-fourth, orange wool; remainder, black wool
RIBBING:	Flat gold tinsel, oval gold tinsel, and silver wire
HACKLE:	Reddish brown spey hackle
THROAT:	Widgeon (or mallard or teal substitute)
WING:	Two strips of brown mallard
HEAD:	Black tying thread

Lady Caroline

THREAD:	Black, prewaxed 6/0
TAIL:	Strands of red golden pheasant breast feather
BODY:	One strand of olive green and two strands of light brown wool wound together side by side
RIBBING:	Flat gold tinsel, oval silver and gold wire
HACKLE:	Gray heron hackle
THROAT:	Golden pheasant breast feather (reddish orange)
WING:	Two strips of brown mallard
HEAD:	Black tying thread

Orange Heron

THREAD:	Red, prewaxed 6/0
BODY:	Rear two-thirds, orange floss; remainder, orange seal's fur (or Seal-Ex)
RIBBING:	Flat and oval silver tinsel
HACKLE:	Gray heron wound from second turn of tinsel
THROAT:	Teal flank feather
WING:	Four hot-orange hackle tips set back to back, and low
HEAD:	Red tying thread

Purple King

THREAD:	Black, prewaxed 6/0
BODY:	Purple wool
RIBBING:	Flat gold tinsel, lilac floss, and gold wire
HACKLE:	Bronze black spey hackle
THROAT:	Teal flank feather
WING:	Two strips of brown mallard
HEAD:	Black tying thread

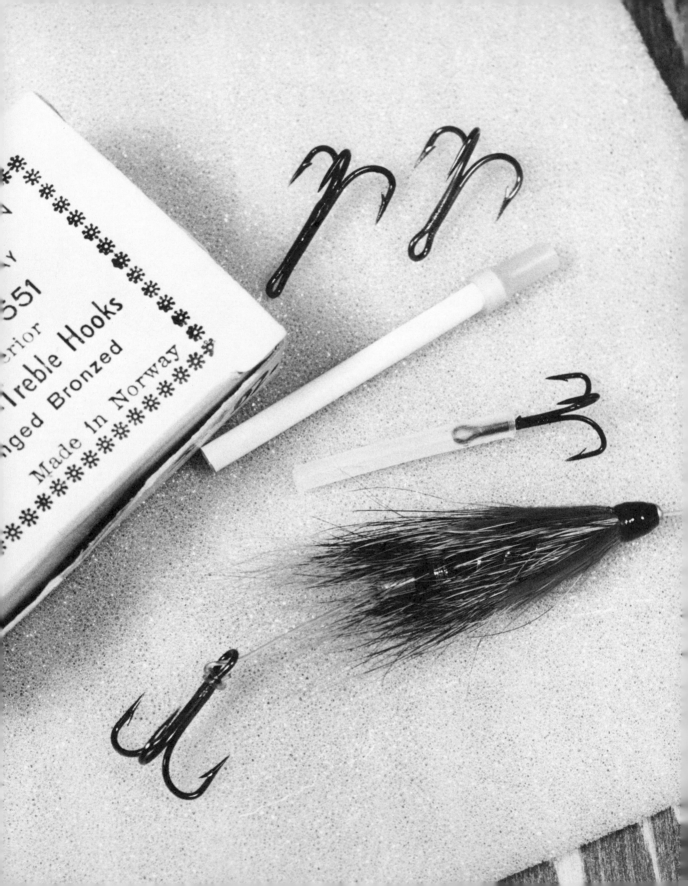

11

Tube Flies

Tube flies were originated in England and became very popular in the late fifties. Unfortunately, they have never really caught on in North America because treble hooks are illegal on many of our rivers. But in Europe and Iceland they are used more frequently than ever.

The advantages of tube flies are many. First of all, they are about the simplest of salmon flies to dress. In many cases they consist of nothing more than some hair tied around the tube in front so that it extends past the posterior end. It's the kind of artificial a fly tier can let his imagination run wild with.

In the beginning of the tube flies' existence they were dressed on almost anything that was hollow, would slip on the leader, and was thin enough, such as small pieces of hollowed-out quill stem, plastic drinking straws, etc. Even today I use tubes that I make myself from hobby shop brass, aluminum, and plastic, of which the shops have a wide variety. It's best, however, to use the ones that are now specifically designed for the purpose, some of which are described in chapter 1. Another distinct advantage of tube flies is that they can be dressed in rather large sizes without having to worry about the weight that often causes difficulties when casting a big fly. Lastly, the sink rate can easily be regulated by choosing either plastic, aluminum, or brass tubes.

Any of the popular salmon flies can be dressed as a tube fly simply by using hair instead of feathers in the wing and by simplifying the body. The important thing is to maintain the same color scheme as that of the fly being converted.

Dressing the Hairy Mary

(Tube Fly)

TUBE: Type C, 1¼" aluminum

THREAD: Black, prewaxed 6/0

BODY: Black silk floss or rayon

RIBBING: Oval gold tinsel

WING: Light red fox squirrel tail

HACKLE: Blue dyed

HEAD: Black tying thread

The Hairy Mary can also be tied on any other size tube, depending on when and where the fly is to be fished. For this size tube a size 8 or 10 treble hook would be fitting, sometimes with a blue hackle wound sparingly as a collar on the shank close to the eye.

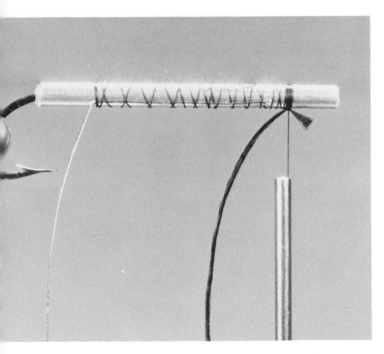

1. To hold the tube while it is being dressed, I cut away the eye of a hook with a shank diameter that will fit snugly inside the tube. Press the tube on tightly so it won't turn, and attach the tying thread. Tie in a four-inch length of medium oval gold tinsel. Wind the tying thread to the left, binding the tinsel down on the tube in the process. The thread should be wound to about a quarter of an inch from the posterior end. Now wind the thread back to the front and tie in a six-inch length of black floss about three-sixteenths inch from the front. This gives you room for the wing, hackle, and head, which are tied in later.

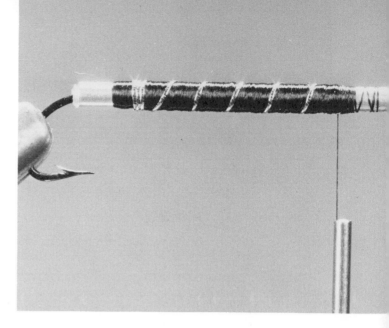

2. Wind the floss on the tube to the left. When it reaches the tinsel, take a couple of turns of floss to the left of it while holding it out of the way. Continue by winding the floss to the right past the tinsel, over the first layer, and tie it off in front. Now take two or three turns of ribbing close together, each turn applied to the right of the previous one. Pull the windings tight and proceed by spiraling the ribbing forward over the body to the front, taking the customary five turns. Tie off the tinsel and trim the surplus ends of tinsel and floss.

3. Cut a bunch of hair from a squirrel tail and remove the fuzz and short hair. Make sure the tip ends are even. They can be tied in two ways: (1) by holding the hair on top of the tube and then pressing the hair around so that it covers the entire circumference before it is fastened with several tight turns of tying thread; or (2) by applying a small bunch at a time. If the latter method is used, the tube should be turned a little after each bunch is tied in and the butt ends trimmed as you go along. The hair should be spread thinly and evenly with either method, and the tips of the hair should project half a body length beyond the posterior end of the tube. This work should be done with as few turns of thread as possible or the head will be too big.

When the hair is in place, the blue-dyed hackle fibers are tied on in the same manner—a few fibers at a time, very sparingly. When all the surplus ends are trimmed, you should wind a short head and apply some head cement.

4. The treble hook with optional hackle collar tied in. The tube body should now be removed from the tying hook and threaded onto the leader attached to the treble hook, and the tube fly is ready to be fished.

5. A small piece of silicone hose can be attached in the rear of the tube, where the treble hook can be inserted after it's tied to the leader to keep it straight when being fished.

SELECTED TUBE FLY DRESSINGS

The patterns I have selected can be dressed on any one of the various tubes described in chapter 1, unless otherwise specified.

Blue Charm

(Tube Fly)

THREAD:	Black, prewaxed 6/0
BODY:	Black silk floss
RIBBING:	Oval silver tinsel
WING:	Gray squirrel tail set as a collar
THROAT:	Blue-dyed hackle wound as a collar and extending one-third down the wing
HEAD:	Black tying thread

Bucktail Tube Fly

TUBE:	Clear
THREAD:	Black, prewaxed 6/0
BODY:	The clear tube
WING:	Bucktail dyed either yellow, hot orange, red, black, green, orange, or purple
HEAD:	Black tying thread

March Brown

(Tube Fly)

THREAD:	Black, prewaxed 6/0
BODY:	Medium brown Seal-Ex dubbing
RIBBING:	Oval gold tinsel

| WING: | Hair from a red fox squirrel tail |
| THROAT: | Brownish partridge body feather wound as a collar and extending one-third down the wing |

Mickey Finn

(Tube Fly)

THREAD:	Black, prewaxed 6/0
BODY:	Flat silver tinsel
RIBBING:	Oval silver tinsel
WING:	Yellow and red dyed bucktail or polar bear hair, mixed and set as a collar

Red Butt

(Tube Fly)

THREAD:	Red, prewaxed 6/0
BUTT:	Shredded red crewel wool or Seal-Ex dubbing
BODY:	Black silk floss
RIBBING:	Oval silver tinsel
WING:	Soft black squirrel tail hair set as a collar
THROAT:	Speckled guinea fowl body feather wound as a collar and extending one-third down the wing
HEAD:	Red tying thread

Silver Wilkinson

(Tube Fly)

| THREAD: | Black, prewaxed 6/0 |
| BUTT: | Shredded red crewel wool or Seal-Ex dubbing |

BODY: Flat silver tinsel

RIBBING: Oval silver tinsel

WING: Bucktail or polar bear hair dyed magenta and set as a collar

THROAT: Teal body feather wound as a collar and extending one-third down the wing

HEAD: Black tying thread

Index of Flies